LSAT Hacks

LSAT Preptest 73 Explanations

A Study Guide for LSAT 73
(September 2014 LSAT)

Graeme Blake

Blake Publications
Montreal, Canada

www.lsathacks.com

ISBN 13: 978-1-927997-08-6
ISBN 10: 1-927997-08-9

Testimonials

Self-study is my preferred way to prep, but I often felt myself missing a few questions each test. Especially for Logic Games, I wanted to see those key inferences which I just couldn't seem to spot on my own. That's where *LSAT Hacks* came in. These solutions have been a tremendous help for my prep, and in training myself to think the way an experienced test taker would.

- **Spencer B.**

Graeme paraphrases the question in plain terms, and walks through each step in obtaining the right answer in a very logical way. This book uses the same techniques as other guides, but its so much more consistent and concise! By the time you read through all the tests, you've gradually developed your eye for the questions. Using this book is a great way to test your mastery of techniques!

- **Sara L.**

Graeme's explanations have the most logical and understandable layout I've seen in an LSAT prep book. The explanations are straightforward and easy to understand, to the point where they make you smack your forehead and say 'of course!

- **Michelle V.**

"Graeme is someone who clearly demonstrates not only LSAT mastery, but the ability to explain it in a compelling manner. This book is an excellent addition to whatever arsenal you're amassing to tackle the LSAT."

- **J.Y. Ping, 7Sage LSAT,**
www.7Sage.com

I did not go through every single answer but rather used the explanations to see if they could explain why my answer was wrong and the other correct. I thought the breakdown of "Type", "Conclusion", "Reasoning" and "Analysis" was extremely useful in simplifying the question. As for quality of the explanations I'd give them a 10 out of 10.

- **Christian F.**

LSAT PrepTests come with answer keys, but it isn't sufficient to know whether or not you picked the credited choice to any given question. The key to making significant gains on this test is understanding the logic underlying the questions.

This is where Graeme's explanations really shine. You may wonder whether your reasoning for a specific question is sound. For the particularly challenging questions, you may be at a complete loss as to how they should be approached.

Having these questions explained by Graeme who scored a 177 on the test is akin to hiring an elite tutor at a fraction of the price. These straightforward explanations will help you improve your performance and, more fundamentally, enhance your overall grasp of the test content.

- **Morley Tatro, Cambridge LSAT,**
www.cambridgelsat.com

Through his conversational tone, helpful introductions, and general recommendations and tips, Graeme Blake has created an enormously helpful companion volume to *The Next Ten Actual Official LSATs*. He strikes a nice balance between providing the clarity and basic explanation of the questions that is needed for a beginner and describing the more complicated techniques that are necessary for a more advanced student.

Even though the subject matter can be quite dry, Graeme succeeds in making his explanations fun and lighthearted. This is crucial: studying for the LSAT is a daunting and arduous task. By injecting some humor and keeping a casual tone, the painful process of mastering the LSAT becomes a little less painful.

When you use *LSAT Hacks* in your studying, you will feel like you have a fun and knowledgeable tutor guiding you along the way.

- **Law Schuelke, LSAT Tutor,**
www.lawLSAT.com

Graeme's explanations are clear, concise and extremely helpful. They've seriously helped me increase my understanding of the LSAT material!

- Jason H.

Graeme's book brings a different view to demystifying the LSAT. The book not only explains the right and wrong answers, but teaches you how to read the reading comprehension and the logical reasoning questions. His technique to set up the games rule by rule help me not making any fatal mistakes in the set up. The strategies he teaches can be useful for someone starting as much as for someone wanting to perfect his strategies. Without his help my LSAT score would have been average, he brought my understanding of the LSAT and my score to a higher level even if english is not my mother tongue.

- Patrick Du.

This book is a must buy for any who are looking to pass or improve their LSAT, I highly recommend it.

- Patrick Da.

This book was really useful to help me understand the questions that I had more difficulty on. When I was not sure as to why the answer to a certain question was that one, the explanations helped me understand where and why I missed the right answer in the first place. I recommend this book to anyone who would like to better understand the mistakes they make.

- Pamela G.

Graeme's book is filled with thoughtful and helpful suggestions on how to strategize for the LSAT test. It is well-organized and provides concise explanations and is definitely a good companion for LSAT preparation.

- Lydia L.

The explanations are amazing, great job. I can hear your voice in my head as I read through the text.

- Shawn M.

LSAT Hacks, especially the logic games sections, was extremely helpful to my LSAT preparation.

The one downside to self study is that sometimes we do not know why we got a question wrong and thus find it hard to move forward. Graeme's book fixes that; it offers explanations and allows you to see where you went wrong. This is an extremely helpful tool and I'd recommend it to anybody that's looking for an additional study supplement.

- Joseph C.

Regardless of how well you're scoring on the LSAT, this book is very helpful. I used it for LR and RC. It breaks down and analyzes each question without the distraction of classification and complicated methods you'll find in some strategy books. Instead of using step-by-step procedures for each question, the analyses focus on using basic critical thinking skills and common sense that point your intuition in the right direction. Even for questions you're getting right, it still helps reinforce the correct thought process. A must-have companion for reviewing prep tests.

- Christine Y.

Take a thorough mastery of the test, an easygoing demeanor, and a genuine desire to help, and you've got a solid resource for fine-tuning your approach when you're tirelessly plowing through test after test. Written from the perspective of a test-taker, this book should help guide your entire thought process for each question, start to finish.

- Yoni Stratievsky, Harvard Ready,
www.harvardready.com

This LSAT guide is the best tool I could have when preparing for the LSAT. Not only does Graeme do a great job of explaining the sections as a whole, he also offers brilliant explanations for each question. He takes the time to explain why an answer is wrong, which is far more helpful when trying to form a studying pattern.

- Amelia F.

LSAT 73 Explanations
Table Of Contents

Introduction

The LSAT is a hard test.

The only people who take the LSAT are smart people who did well in University. The LSAT takes the very best students, and forces them to compete.

If the test's difficulty shocked you, this is why. The LSAT is a test designed to be hard for smart people.

That's the bad news. But there's hope. The LSAT is a *standardized* test. It has patterns. It can be learned.

To get better, you have to review your mistakes. Many students write tests and move on, without fully understanding their mistakes.

This is understandable. The LSAC doesn't publish official explanations for most tests. It's hard to be sure why you were wrong.

That's where this book comes in. It's a companion for LSAT 73, the September 2014 LSAT.

This book lets you see where you went wrong. It has a full walk through of each question and of every answer choice. You can use this book to fix your mistakes, and make sure you understand *everything*.

By getting this book, you've shown that you're serious about beating this test. I sincerely hope it helps you get the score you want.

There are a few things that I'd like to highlight.

Logical Reasoning: It can be hard to identify conclusions in LR. You don't get feedback on whether you identified the conclusion correctly.

This book gives you that feedback. I've identified the conclusion and the reasoning for each argument. Try to find these on your own beforehand, and make sure they match mine.

Logic Games: Do the game on your own before looking at my explanation. You can't think about a game unless you're familiar with the rules. Once you read my explanations, draw my diagrams yourself on a sheet of paper. You'll understand them much better by recopying them.

Reading Comprehension: You should form a mental map of the passage. This helps you locate details quickly. Make a 1-2 line summary of each paragraph (it can be a mental summary).

I've written my own summaries for each passage. They show the minimum amount of information that you should know after reading a passage, without looking back.

I've included line references in my explanations. You do not need to check these each time. They're only there in case you aren't sure where something is.

Do these three things, and you can answer most Reading Comprehension questions with ease.:

1. Know the point of the passage.
2. Understand the passage, in broad terms. Reread anything you don't understand.
3. Know where to find details. That's the point of the paragraph summaries. I usually do mine in my head, and they're shorter than what I've written.

Review This Book

Before we start, I'd like to ask you a favor. I'm an independent LSAT instructor. I don't have a marketing budget.

But I do my best to make good guides to the LSAT. If you agree, I would love it if you took two minutes to write a review on amazon.com

People judge a book by its reviews. So if you like this guide you can help others discover it. I'd be very grateful.

Good luck!

Graeme

p.s. I'm a real person, and I want to know how the LSAT goes and what you think of this book. Send me an email at graeme@lsathacks.com!

p.p.s. For more books, check out the further reading section at the back. I'm also offering a free half hour LSAT lesson if you fill out a survey.

How To Use This Book

The word "Hacks" in the title is meant in the sense used by the tech world and Lifehacker: "solving a problem" or "finding a better way".

The LSAT can be beaten, but you need a good method. My goal is for you to use this book to understand your mistakes and master the LSAT.

This book is *not* a replacement for practicing LSAT questions on your own.

You have to try the questions by yourself first. When you review, try to see why you were wrong *before* you look at my explanations.

Active review will teach you to fix your own mistakes. The explanations are there for when you have difficulty solving on a question on your own or when you want another perspective on a question.

When you *do* use the explanations, have the question on hand. These explanations are not meant to be read alone. You should use them to help you think about the questions more deeply.

Most of the logical reasoning explanations are pretty straightforward. Necessary assumption questions are often an exception, so I want to give you some guidance to help you interpret the explanations.

The easiest way to test the right answer on a necessary assumption question is to "negate" it.

You negate a statement by making it false, in the slightest possible way. For example, the negation of "The Yankees will win all their games" is "The Yankees will *not* win all their games (they will lose at least one)."

You *don't* have to say that the Yankees will lose *every* game. That goes too far.

If the negation of an answer choice proves the conclusion wrong, then that answer is *necessary* to the argument, and it's the correct answer.

Often, I negate the answer choices when explaining necessary assumption questions, so just keep in mind why they're negated.

Logic games also deserve special mention.

Diagramming is a special symbolic language that you have to get comfortable with to succeed.

If you just *look* at my diagrams without making them yourself, you may find it hard to follow along. You can only learn a language by using it yourself.

So you will learn *much* more if you draw the diagrams on your own. Once you've seen how I do a setup, try to do it again by yourself.

With constant practice, you *will* get better at diagramming, and soon it will come naturally.

But you must try on your own. Draw the diagrams.

Note that when you draw your own diagrams, you don't have to copy every detail from mine. For example, I often leave off the numbers when I do linear games. I've included them in the book, because they make it easier for you to follow along.

But under timed conditions, I leave out many details so that I can draw diagrams faster. If you practice making drawings with fewer details, they become just as easy to understand.

Keep diagrams as minimal as possible.

If you simply don't *like* the way I draw a certain rule type, then you can substitute in your own style of diagram. Lots of people succeed using different styles of drawing.

Just make sure your replacement is easy to draw consistently, and that the logical effect is the same. I've chosen these diagrams because they are clear, they're easy to draw, and they *keep you from forgetting rules.*

I've included line references to justify Reading Comprehension Answers. Use these only in case you're unsure about an explanation. You don't have to go back to the passage for every line reference.

Short Guide to Logical Reasoning

LR Question Types

Must be True: The correct answer is true.

Most Strongly Supported: The correct answer is probably true.

Strengthen/Weaken: The answer is correct if it even slightly strengthens/weakens the argument.

Parallel Reasoning: The correct answer will mirror the argument's structure exactly. It is often useful to diagram these questions (but not always).

Sufficient Assumption: The correct answer will prove the conclusion. It's often useful to diagram sufficient assumption questions. For example:

The conclusion is: A → D

There is a gap between premises and conclusion:

A   B → C → D   **missing link:** A → B or ~~B~~ → ~~A~~

A → B → C   D   **missing link:** C → D or ~~D~~ → ~~C~~

A → B   C → D   **missing link:** B → C or ~~C~~ → ~~B~~

The right answer will provide the missing link.

Necessary Assumption: The correct answer will be essential to the argument's conclusion. Use the negation technique: If the correct answer is false (negated), then the argument falls apart.
The negation of hot is "not hot" rather than cold.

Here's how to do negations: You just make the idea false. This is not so much about grammar as it is about thinking what the idea is, and a counterexample. E.g.

"All Americans are nice" → "One guy in Arkansas named Bob is sort of mean. Every single other American is always really nice"

The "grammatical" negation is "not all Americans are nice", but it's so much clearer and easier to think in terms of making the idea not true.

Point at Issue: Point at Issue questions require two things. **1.** The two speakers must express an opinion on something. **2.** They must disagree about it.

Flawed Reasoning: The correct answer will be a description of a reasoning error made in the argument. It will often be worded very abstractly.

Practice understanding the answers, right and wrong. Flawed Reasoning answers are very abstract, but they all mean something. Think of examples to make them concrete and easier to understand.

Basic Logic

Take the phrase: "All cats have tails."

"Cats" is the sufficient condition. Knowing that something is a cat is "sufficient" for us to say that it has a tail. "Tails" is a necessary condition, because you can't be a cat without a tail. You can draw this sentence as $C \rightarrow T$

The **contrapositive** is a correct logical deduction, and reads "anything without a tail is not a cat." You can draw this as $\not{T} \rightarrow \not{C}$. Notice that the terms are reversed, and negated.

Incorrect Reversal: "Anything with a tail is a cat." This is a common logical error on the LSAT.

$T \rightarrow C$ (Wrong! Dogs have tails and aren't cats.)

Incorrect Negation: "If it is not a cat, it doesn't have a tail." This is another common error.

$\not{C} \rightarrow \not{T}$ (Wrong! Dogs aren't cats, but have tails.)

General Advice: Always remember what you are looking for on each question. The correct answer on a strengthen question would be incorrect on a weaken question.

Watch out for subtle shifts in emphasis between the stimulus and the incorrect answer choices. An example would be the difference between "how things are" and "how things should be."

Justify your answers. If you're tempted to choose an answer choice that says something like the sentence below, then be sure you can fill in the blank:

Answer Choice Says: "The politician attacked his opponents' characters",

Fill In The Blank: "The politician said __________ about his opponents' characters."

If you cannot say what the attack was, you can't pick that answer. This applies to many things. You must be able to show that the stimulus supports your idea.

A Few Logic Games Tips

Rule 1: When following along with my explanations....draw the diagrams yourself, too!

This book will be much more useful if you try the games by yourself first. You must think through games on your own, and no book will do that for you. You must have your mind in a game to solve it.

Use the explanations when you find a game you can't understand on your own, or when you want to know how to solve a game more efficiently.

Some of the solutions may seem impossible to get on your own. It's a matter of practice. When you learn how to solve one game efficiently, solving other games becomes easier too.

Try to do the following when you solve games:

Work With What Is Definite: Focus on what must be true. Don't figure out every possibility.

Draw Your Deductions: Unsuccessful students often make the same deductions as successful students. But the unsuccessful students forget their deductions, 15 seconds later! I watch this happen.

Draw your deductions, or you'll forget them. Don't be arrogant and think this doesn't happen to you. It would happen to *me* if I didn't draw my deductions.

Draw Clear Diagrams: Many students waste time looking back and forth between confusing pictures. They've done everything right, but can't figure out their own drawings!

You should be able to figure out your drawings 3 weeks later. If you can't, then they aren't clear enough. I'm serious: look back at your old drawings. Can you understand them? If not, you need a more consistent, cleaner system.

Draw Local Rules: When a question gives you a new rule (a local rule), draw it. Then look for deductions by combining the new rule with your existing rules. Then double-check what you're being asked and see if your deduction is the right answer. This works 90% of the time for local rule questions. And it's fast.

If you don't think you have time to draw diagrams for each question, practice drawing them faster. It's a learnable skill, and it pays off.

Try To Eliminate a Few Easy Answer Choices First: You'll see examples in the explanations that show how certain deductions will quickly get rid of 1-3 answer choices on many questions. This saves time for harder answer choices and it frees up mental space.

You don't have to try the answer choices in order, without thinking about them first.

Split Games Into Two Scenarios When Appropriate: If a rule only allows something to be one of two ways (e.g. F is in 1 or 7), then draw two diagrams: one with F in 1, and one with F in 7. This leads to extra deductions surprisingly often. And it always makes the game easier to visualize.

Combine Rules To Make Deductions: Look for variables that appear in multiple rules. These can often be combined. Sometimes there are no deductions, but it's a crime not to look for them.

Reread The Rules: Once you've made your diagram, reread the rules. This lets you catch any mistakes, which are fatal. It doesn't take very long, and it helps you get more familiar with the rules.

Draw Rules Directly On The Diagram: Mental space is limited. Three rules are much harder to remember than two. When possible, draw rules on the diagram so you don't have to remember them.

Memorize Your Rules: You should memorize every rule you can't draw on the diagram. It doesn't take long, you'll go faster, and you'll make fewer mistakes. Try it, it's not that hard.

If you spend 30 seconds doing this, you'll often save a minute by going through the game faster.

You should also make a numbered list of rules that aren't on the diagram, in case you need to check them.

Section I – Reading Comprehension

Passage 1 – Natural Selection

Questions 1–7

Paragraph Summaries

1. Strict constructionist Darwinians contradict Darwin by saying that natural selection explains all evolution.
2. Strict constructionism implies that every attribute of every species is due to adaptation. But nature provides many counterexamples.
3. Many DNA mutations are random, and have no effect on survival. Nonetheless they persist and are passed down. This is a change in species which has nothing to do with natural selection.
4. Massive catastrophes let some species succeed even though they were not adapted to their original environments.

Analysis

The author's opinion is very important on this passage. They think the strict constructionists are wrong. This is clear from the first paragraph. The author says strict constructionists contradict Darwin himself.

You may have noticed that the author doesn't give *any* evidence supporting the strict constructionists. And after presenting the strict constructionist position, the author does nothing but criticize strict constructionism, by showing evidence against it. This is a strong sign. The author thinks the strict constructionists are really, really wrong.

The first two paragraphs are spent describing the strict constructionists views. The final two paragraphs provide examples that show why the strict constructionists are wrong.

It's necessary to understand a little about natural selection. That's the idea that individual members of a species will reproduce more if they are adapted to their environment. Their offspring will share their traits, and over time, those characteristics become more common in that species.

The standard example is a species of moth that was common during the industrial revolution in England. As pollution darkened the landscape, the moths became darker, because this allowed them to blend in with the landscape and avoided predators. As pollution diminished in the 20th century, the moths became lighter again.

The author agrees that natural selection is a factor in evolution (lines 1-4, lines 23-27), but their point is that it's not the *only* factor.

Paragraph three shows how species can be changed by random, neutral mutations that are passed down and that change species over time. The mutations offer no reproductive advantage, so natural selection plays no role in their transmission.

The fourth paragraph gives the example of the mammals. We took over the world after the asteroid strike killed off the dinosaurs. But our takeover didn't happen because we were particularly well adapted at the time of the asteroid strike. It was just dumb luck that we were small enough to survive.

We had a selection advantage *after* the asteroid strike, but natural selection doesn't explain how we originally arrived in the position of being in the right place at the right time.

Question 1

DISCUSSION: The main point is that the strict constructionists are wrong to say that natural selection is the only means of evolution.

A. CORRECT. The two areas of science are paragraphs 3 and 4. This supports the author's main opinion, stated in lines 19-22: the strict constructionists are wrong.

B. Nonsense. See lines 16-22: "If the strict constructionists are right....but in fact" The author *disagrees* with the strict constructionists.

C. This describes paragraph 3. That paragraph is just evidence supporting the author's main point. The main point is that the strict constructionists are wrong.

D. This is *true*. But truth is not enough for the main point. This is just a fact stated in the opening paragraph. The main point is that the author disagrees with the strict constructionists.

E. This goes too far. The author's point was that *not all* evolution comes from natural selection. They never said that natural selection has no impact on the survival of species.

Question 2

DISCUSSION: The survival of mammals was described in the fourth paragraph. This type of question has a precise answer that you can find in the passage. Meanwhile, the answer choices are specifically constructed to confuse you. Don't look at them.

Instead, go back to the fourth paragraph, and see what it says. With practice, you can find the answer to questions like this in less than five seconds. You'll save time you would have spent deciding between misleading answer choices.

A. The fourth paragraph says mammals *weren't* adapted. We survived due to dumb luck (lines 54-57).

B. CORRECT. Lines 43-48 say this directly.

C. The passage never said that mammals were intelligent. This answer is just playing to your existing belief that mammals are intelligent because you're a mammal.

D. The passage never says that mammals used to live in a wide range of environments. This answer is trying to make you use your outside knowledge that mammals *currently* live in a wide range of environments.

E. The passage never mentions mammalian reproduction. Maybe you were thinking of rabbits?

Question 3

DISCUSSION: Genetic mutations are in paragraph three. It's a good idea to go back and skim that paragraph before looking at the answers. Shouldn't take more than 5-10 seconds.

The point of doing this is to have *all* the information about genetic mutations fresh at hand. This lets you quickly eliminate nonsense answers.

A. The author never said how many mutations are passed down.
B. This just combines paragraph 3 and paragraph 4 in a weird way. The author never said there's a link between mass extinctions and genetic mutations.
C. The author never mentions whether mutations change behavior or appearance.
D. CORRECT. Lines 27-28 say this directly. ("Neither category" means most mutations aren't helpful or harmful for reproduction.)
E. Large and small species are an idea from paragraph 4, which deals with mass extinctions. The author never mentioned large and small in relation to mutations.

Question 4

DISCUSSION: As usual, the right answer is stated in the passage. The wrong answers contradict the passage or quote familiar words out of context.

Questions like this reward your ability to retain details or know where they were mentioned. The better you know the passage, the more the wrong answers will appear obviously wrong.

After reading the passage, I always skim it before starting. This lets me see all text at least twice, and I retain significantly more detail.

A. This is far too strong. The author's point was only that natural selection is not responsible for *all* changes.
B. CORRECT. Paragraph 4 says this. We mammals flourished after the asteroid strike 65 million years ago, even though we had not been adapted to our environment.
C. This contradicts lines 29-31: most changes have no advantage or disadvantage.
D. Lines 43-45 say that large animals have difficulty surviving "catastrophic" conditions. But that's not the same thing as "harsh" conditions. The arctic or a desert are harsh environments, but they're not "catastrophic".
E. Line 11 mentions form and behavior. It doesn't distinguish between the two ideas. This answer is trying to fool you by mentioning words you might remember from the passage, out of context.

Question 5

DISCUSSION: The author is unusually critical of the strict constructionists. See lines 1-9 and 16-21. The strict constructionists contradict Darwin (usually a mistake) and there is ample evidence their view is wrong.

The author also gives *no* evidence supporting the strict constructionists. They merely describe the strict constructionist views and proceed to prove them wrong.

So the correct answer will be something like "clear disagreement".

A. CORRECT. See the analysis above. "Emphatic" means: with emphasis, clear.
B. Too weak. The author doesn't say a single good thing about the strict constructionists. The author thinks they're entirely wrong.
C. Nonsense. The author spends most of the passage disagreeing with the strict constructionists. The author definitely isn't neutral.
D. Rubbish. The author doesn't say a single nice thing about the strict constructionists, and the author disagrees with them frequently. See the analysis above.
E. Even worse than D. This suggests the author completely agrees with the strict constructions. The opposite is true: they completely disagree. See the analysis above.

Question 6

DISCUSSION: Before you answer a question like this, you should reread/skim the second paragraph. Should only take 5-10 seconds to refresh yourself on what it says.

Then you're fully prepared and can answer the question faster. Ultimately, rereading/skimming before answering saves time.

The point of the second paragraph is this: the author elaborates on the strict constructionist view and the consequences of that view. Then the author shows they disagree with the strict constructionists.

A. Actually, the author never mentioned *why* the strict constructionists disagree with evolutionary theory. No objections are listed.
B. Not quite. The third paragraph lists recent evidence. The second paragraph just describes the strict constructionist views and says they are disproven by evidence that is to follow.
C. The author never says whether the evidence in paragraphs 3 and 4 has gotten much attention.
D. The author actually never says what arguments exist in support of the strict constructionist position.
E. CORRECT. This refers specifically to lines 16-19. "Ramifications" means the consequences of the view of the strict constructionists, if that view is correct.
Since we know the consequences of their view, we can disprove their view if we show the consequences are false. That's the purpose of lines 21-24 + paragraphs 3 and 4.
This answer covers everything well, but it's unusually vaguely worded.

Question 7

DISCUSSION: The point of the passage is to prove that the strict constructionists are wrong. See lines 21-24.

A. What recently proposed hypothesis? “The strict constructionists are wrong” is not a hypothesis. It’s a claim *against* a hypothesis.

B. There’s no debate. The answer instead relentlessly argues that the strict constructionists are wrong.

C. **CORRECT.** The whole point of the passage is to show that the strict constructionists are wrong. See especially lines 21-24.

D. The author didn’t personally criticize strict constructionists. They just said the strict constructionist *theory* is wrong. Criticizing proponents would be: Strict constructions are immoral, strict constructionists smell bad, etc.

E. The author never said whether strict constructionism is popular.

Passage 2 – Julia Margaret Cameron
Questions 8–15

Paragraph Summaries

1. The charm of Julia Margaret Cameron's pictures is that they were "flawed" due to the difficult conditions under which they were taken.
2. The photos are very human, we can see the struggles of sitting. It's impossible to suspend our disbelief while looking at the photographs.
3. *The Passing of Arthur* shows how Cameron's photographs could be both amateur and artistic.

Analysis

The little grey text at the top of the passage is important. This is a passage about *Victorian* photographer Julia Margaret Cameron. The Victorian period was during the reign of Queen Victoria, roughly 1837-1901. So these photos are *old.*

You've surely seen photos of camera from back then. They were enormous, on big fixed stands. You had to sit very still, otherwise the photos blurred. That's one reason everyone looked so serious in old photographs.

Julia Margaret Cameron took photos of scenes from theatre, art and religion. But she did so at a time when taking pictures was hard. A central element of the passage is that it was rather difficult to photograph the scenes she wanted.

So we get all kinds of comical side effects. Instead of grand historical figures, we see our uncle who can never stop blinking during family portraits (I'm making up an example). You may have been through long, hard family portraits. Imagine doing it in Shakespearean costume and trying to look heroic.

Julia Margaret Cameron's aim was to make serious artistic photographs (lines 15-16). But she failed. Instead she made humorous, human photos that show us as we are.

And her photographs succeed *because* of this human element. See lines 15-20. However, Cameron's photographs could be moving as well. The third paragraphs expands on this point. If the photographs were merely amateur, they would not be interesting (see lines 45-46). Cameron's photograph of the *Passing of Arthur* is both amateur *and* majestic.

Overall, the author really likes Cameron's photographs. The fact that she partly failed and partly succeeded in her aim of making serious art is what makes the photographs special.

Lines 14-16 and lines 43-46 are the most significant in the passage. In lines 14-16, we learn that Cameron was *trying* to make serious works of art. She hadn't wanted to making goofy photographs. In lines 43-46 we learn that the author thinks Cameron's work succeeded because it was part amateur, but also partly artistic.

Often, a couple of key lines distill the author's opinion. Those two sections come up in almost all questions. Clearly, the LSAC expected you to miss those points. If you have a clear view of the author's believes it gives you a frame of reference through which to interpret the answers.

Question 8

DISCUSSION: The main point of the passage is to describe Julia Margaret Cameron's photography and why it is effective.

Lines 43-46 are very significant. These show that the author liked Cameron's photographs, and that the combination of sloppy sitting but high purpose is what makes them great.

A. This is just a fact that supports the main idea. The author does think the photographs were comical, but they also think they were more than comical. See lines 43-46.
B. CORRECT. There's no single place the passage says this, but it's the main point. See for example lines 36-38 (our awareness of doubleness) and lines 43-46 (the photos quality comes from their dual nature).
C. This answer contradicts the passage. Cameron's photographs didn't have an "implicit" claim to be compared with the masterpieces of Western painting. The claim was explicit; Cameron was *trying* to make photographs that were as artistically significant as the great paintings. See lines 15-16 and line 10.
But the behavior of the sitters doesn't undermine the photographs – the author thinks that's what gives them their charm. See lines 43-46.
D. The author disagrees with this. See lines 43-46. Amateurism is part of what makes Cameron's photos great.
E. This contradicts lines 43-46. The artistry of the photos is an important element.

Question 9

DISCUSSION: The props are mentioned in the fourth paragraph. Lines 43-46 are especially important. The author thinks that both the amateurism and the art of the photographs is what makes them great.

The props were an amateur element. We know the mast is a broomstick, for example.

A. CORRECT. See the analysis above.
B. The transformative power of theatre is only mentioned in lines 38-40.
C. The props were not intentionally bad. While they add to the charm, the charm was unintentional. Remember, Cameron was trying to make serious works of art (lines 14-16). So we can't credit Cameron's ingenuity for the charm of the amateur props.
D. Cameron had not intended her props to be ridiculous. See lines 14-16.
E. See line 50. The goofy props are an insignificant detail.

Question 10

DISCUSSION: You should reread around lines 34-36. The passage says that when you see a painting that tells a story, you can pretend the story is real. But you cannot pretend a photograph is real.

There's no obvious prephrase for this question. Instead, think about what it's like to look at paintings vs. photographs and keep your mind open.

A. When we suspend our disbelief in front of a painting, we're looking at the finished product. It doesn't matter to us how long it took to paint the subjects in the painting.

B. This is something *true* about paintings, but it doesn't explain anything. If a situation in a painting is obviously impossible, then why do we suspend our disbelief and pretend it's real?

C. This is similar to A. When we look at a painting, we have no idea how long it took to paint. The conditions under which a painting was created don't impact our impressions of the painting.

D. CORRECT. This shows that a painter can reduce contradictory details in a painting. A photographer, on the other hand, has to take their subject as they find them.

I'll give an example: Suppose a sitter playing Hercules has weak legs. The painter can reproduce their strong upper body, but "fix" their legs so they're stronger than in real life. Whereas a photographer has to photograph the legs.

E. A stylistic imprint doesn't explain our reaction to paintings.

Question 11

DISCUSSION: Cameron was trying to make serious works of art. She unintentionally made semi-goofy, semi-artistic photos. This was due to the amateurism of her props and sitters.

For Cameron's intention, see lines 14-16. Cameron had wanted to make "seamless works of art".

A. Here, the playwright intentionally introduces elements. But Cameron *accidentally* introduced amateurism into her pictures.

B. Here, the rap artist *intentionally* subverts the song. But Cameron didn't mean to make goofy photos.

C. CORRECT. The ordinary objects are Cameron's regular people. The certain grandeur is the fact that some of Cameron's photographs had a certain artistry about them (see lines 45-46 and 53-57).

D. Cameron's photographs weren't functional! They were artistic photographs of scenes from history and art.

E. In this case, the director is *trying* to make her work amateur. Cameron wasn't trying.

Question 12

DISCUSSION: All of the wrong answers can be eliminated using the passage, and the right answer contradicts the passage.

Usually it takes to long to check each answer (but if you have the time, you should come back and do so). What you should do instead is check the 1-2 answers you're not sure about.

You can be 90% sure about the right answer, but it's better to check and be 100% sure. Otherwise, mistakes creep in.

A. The passage says this. Painting is less realistic than photography, but only painting allows us to suspend disbelief. See lines 34-36.

B. See lines 43-46. The author thinks that the amateurishness of Cameron's photographs is a good thing.

C. See lines 43-46 and the whole second paragraph. Amateurishness is the incongruity. Also lines 13-16. The author thinks Cameron's work succeeds *because* it has a silly aspect.

D. See lines 38-40. We may believe that actors are real, but perhaps only some of the time.

E. **CORRECT.** See lines 14-20. The author thinks Cameron's work succeeded even though (and because) Cameron failed in her intentions.

Question 13

DISCUSSION: There's no way to prephrase the question. Instead, go through all the answers quickly, then focus more narrowly on those that seem plausible. Check your answer against the passage if possible.

I say to go through all the answers first because often D or E will be obviously right. You don't want to waste 20-30 seconds on A, B or C without looking at all the answers first.

A. We have no idea. The author didn't talk about Victorian photography in general or whether other photographers documented real life.

B. We have no idea. The author just tells us about Cameron, not photographers in general.

C. Nonsense. The passage didn't even mention publicity stills of actors.
(The author did mention photographs of actors on lines 40-42. But we don't know if these were publicity stills, and the passage doesn't say if it's referring to Victorian photos of actors.)

D. We have no idea why Cameron used amateurs. Professional models may or may not have existed.

E. **CORRECT.** Line 31 supports this: "trying desperately hard to sit still". In modern pictures we don't have to try desperately hard. Photos can often be taken quite quickly, and even when we're in motion.

Question 14

DISCUSSION: The author mentions suspension of disbelief in order to contrast photography against other art forms.

We can believe that a painting or actors on stage are real. But we can never believe that a staged photograph of an artistic or historical scene is real.

A. Ridiculous. There aren't even any conclusion words in that part of the passage. It's clear from a read of the entire passage that the author's purpose is to describe and praise Cameron. Their conclusion is essentially on lines 43-46.

B. **CORRECT.** This is a vague answer. I'm not 100% certain how to justify it with a line reference, which is rare.
But the gist of it is correct. The contrast is the difference between narrative paintings vs. photography. We can never believe that Cameron's photographs are real.
But that's what makes them charming (see lines 43-46). Our failure to suspend our disbelief with Cameron's photos is what allows us to both enjoy their humor yet be amazed by their artistic beauty.

C. The author *likes* Cameron's narrative photography. There is no "negative appraisal" – an appraisal is an overall opinion, and the author's overall opinion is positive. See lines 43-46.

D. The author doesn't claim any criticism is "conceptually confused". I have no idea what this answer could refer to.
Criticisms of Cameron are not central to the argument; they're only mentioned in passing, as in lines 53-55.

E. The contrast is narrative photography vs. paintings/drama. Paintings and drama are *similar* in that both allow us to suspend disbelief.

Question 15

DISCUSSION: There's no good way to prephrase primary purpose questions. There are multiple possible answers.

In general, before moving on from a passage, you should have a good idea of what the author thinks and why they say what they say.

In this case, the author likes Cameron. Lines 43-46 come closest to summing up the passage: The mix of amateur/artistic is what makes the photographs interesting.

This question also uses lines 14-20, which tell us that Cameron did not intend to make photos that were a mix of goofy and serious. She wanted to make high art.

A. This isn't it. The passage doesn't say anything about Cameron's development. The main discussion is of Cameron's failure to achieve her artistic goals. (This failure was a good thing, see lines 43-46).

B. **CORRECT.** See lines 14-20 and 43-46. The author likes Cameron's works because they are part amateurish, part artistic.
Lines 14-20 are what justify this answer. Cameron wasn't trying to make amateurish photographs! Her goal was to make serious art. She failed at her goal, but made better pictures as a result.

C. Cameron's vision wasn't necessarily theatrical. She seems to have been inspired by great paintings as much or more than she was inspired by theatre (see lines 6-10).

D. The author isn't interested in saying Cameron failed. The author liked Cameron! See lines 43-46.

E. *The Passing of Arthur* is not the main point of the passage. It's just an example that supports the passage's idea, which is that Cameron's works were interesting because of the amateur/artistic mix seen in works such as *The Passing of Arthur*.

Passage 3 – Marcuse and Advertising
Questions 16–21

Paragraph Summaries

1. Marcuse said advertising makes us believe we are satisfied, when we never can be. Advertising creates false needs that enrich corporations.
2. False needs are created on top of real needs. E.g. We need sex, and we are sold perfume.
3. If Marcuse is right, we cannot actually know what our real needs are, because he says we respond to the persuasion of advertising without thinking.
4. Marcuse is wrong to think we respond to advertising without thinking. Ads can't make us do things we don't want to do. Consumers may consciously be buying products to fulfill their emotional needs.

Analysis

This is a very complex passage. Paragraphs 1 and 2 present Marcuse's argument. Advertising creates false needs. Marcuse says we are no longer able to tell what we truly want. Advertising makes us think we are satisfied, but we live in a world where satisfaction is impossible (lines 6-9).

The third paragraph is where the author starts to disagree with Marcuse. That paragraph is misleading, because the author doesn't actually agree with her own argument in paragraph 3.

In paragraph 3, the author is talking about what would happen *IF* Marcuse is right. If Marcuse is right about false needs, then we have no idea what our real needs are. The forces of persuasion are everywhere, and it's impossible to tell whether a desire is genuine or whether that desire is just something we got unconsciously from an ad.

This is an *internal* flaw to Marcuse's argument. The author is saying that *if* Marcuse is right, then it would be very hard to figure out what's real, because our perceptions would be unconsciously warped.

But the author doesn't think Marcuse is right. The author thinks that adults are usually able to understand the persuasive techniques advertisers use, and respond sensibly (lines 40-44). We don't just passively submit to the suggestions of ads. Lines 35-37 say we respond to ads autonomously. That means we're able to think about them and act of our own free will.

Lines 46-56 show that consumers may get enjoyment from buying things, even if it's not the enjoyment promised.

For instance, suppose a perfume promises you sex, glamour and luxury. You decide to buy the perfume, but not for that reason. You instead expect the perfume will smell nice, and make people treat you a little bit better.

The ad may have helped you decide to buy the perfume, but you weren't fooled into trying to use it to satisfy a "false need". Instead you are using the perfume to satisfy your real needs for a pleasant olfactory environment and to be treated well by others.

This is an example of what "another sort of fulfillment (lines 54-55) refers to.

The rest of the line is also worth thinking about. The author says that it's not true that a product's "genuine fulfillment of needs must be less than the advertisement suggests". For example, a garbage bag might promise that it is easy to tie and never breaks. There's no reason a garbage bag couldn't live up to the promises of the ad.

Reading comprehension passages refer to real situations. You're allowed to use your own experience to help you figure out what the author means. All the words in passages have real meaning.

Question 16

DISCUSSION: The main point of the passage is that Marcuse's critique of advertising is wrong. See lines 35-37.

The author is *only* concerned with critiquing Marcuse. The author doesn't make other claims, and they aren't saying that ads are a good thing.

The third paragraph is interesting....the author doesn't agree with their own argument in that paragraph!

In paragraph 3, the author says that if Marcuse is right, we'll never figure out our real needs. But the author doesn't think this is true. See lines 35-37: consumers are able to consciously respond to advertisements. Lines 40-44 say that we can recognize and respond to the techniques used.

So the third paragraph is not true. The argument in final paragraph is the main point. We're not blind to our real needs. We're able to react independently to ads, and we can purchase products to fulfill real needs.

It's a myth that main point questions need to sum up all the paragraphs. That's often true, but for a passage that's an argument, the real criterion is whether the answer sums up the author's conclusion.

A. The author thinks Marcuse's critique is wrong, but that doesn't mean the author thinks ads are good. If one claim is wrong, the opposite isn't necessarily right.

B. This just sums up paragraph 3. It leaves out paragraph 4, which was the main critique against Marcuse. This answer also ought to have said that consumers are more autonomous than Marcuse thought.

C. **CORRECT.** You might think this only covers the fourth paragraph. But the fourth paragraph was the central conclusion of the argument. Paragraphs 1 and 2 described Marcuse's arguments, "Marcuse's arguments" in this answer allude to those paragraphs.
This answer leaves out paragraph 3, but that paragraph was actually an aside that the author doesn't agree with (see the analysis above for more on that).

D. This isn't even true. We don't know what critics of advertising typically do. This passage is just talking about "some critics" (line 1). We have no idea if most critics of advertising agree with Marcuse.

E. The first half of this answer is good. But then.... "ignores consumers physical and psychological needs"? *Marcuse* was the one who talked about physical and psychological needs, see lines 15-16. This answer is just false.

Question 17

DISCUSSION: This question is asking for something *Marcuse* believes about advertisers. Marcuse's arguments are given in paragraphs 1 and 2, so you should look there.

If possible, find the lines that prove the right answer correct. Most wrong answers on this type of question are pure nonsense that feel familiar because they use words that were mentioned in the passage. But the words are always out of context. An answer is not right just because it feels familiar!

A. The passage never mentions psychological research or how advertisers create manipulative strategies.

B. CORRECT. Lines 16-18 say this directly. "Appropriates" means "uses" in this context.

C. The *author* said this on lines 39-40, but that was their own opinion, not Marcuse's.

D. What does this even refer to? Marcuse never said that consumers have a need for independent decision making or that advertisers refer to that need. This answer is just a weird combination of Marcuse's discussion of needs in paragraph 2 with the author's discussion of decision making in paragraph 4.

E. Marcuse never said what advertisers think about false needs. Maybe they agree with Marcuse, and maybe they don't.
This answer simply isn't in the passage, because Marcuse never talked about it.

Question 18

DISCUSSION: The first paragraph describes Marcuse's theory of advertising.

It's always a good idea to reread/skim the relevant paragraph before answering this type of question. This takes a few seconds, but you'll eliminate wrong answers much faster.

A. What political context? The passage doesn't describe any political systems.

B. If this answer were right, then we'd be able to find something in paragraph 1 that says *how* advertising creates false needs. The first paragraph says Marcuse thinks advertising creates false needs, but Marcuse doesn't say *how* advertising does this in paragraph 1.

C. The first paragraph doesn't say anything like this! The word psychology doesn't even appear, and the paragraph doesn't evaluate the techniques advertising uses.

D. The first paragraph is only talking about "some" critics of advertising: those that agree with Marcuse. We have no idea if they're the dominant critics of advertising.

E. CORRECT. The first paragraph has two parts. Lines 4-15 describe Marcuse's theory of false needs. Lines 1-4 say some critics think this theory is the major explanation of advertising's power. In this answer, that corresponds to "Marcusian views" and "role in certain criticisms of advertising".

Question 19

DISCUSSION: On this sort of question, the passage will usually directly say the right answer.

Rather than spend time "thinking" about which of two answers is right, you're better off just checking the passage to see if it says the answer. If you have a good map of the passage, you can find most facts in 3-5 seconds (this can be practiced).

"Thought" is not useful on this sort of question. Memory recall and ability to locate text is what this type of question tests.

A. CORRECT. Lines 6-11 say this directly.

B. Physical needs are only mentioned on line 16, and Marcuse never says that society fails to satisfy our basic physical needs.
Instead, Marcuse claims that we live in an unsatisfying society (lines 8-9). It's possible to be unsatisfied even if needs are met.

C. This answer is not one of Marcuse's ideas. This is something the author argues would be true if Marcuse were right....it's an *implication* of Marcuse's ideas. People can hold ideas without believing in the implications of their ideas.
e.g. Someone who believes that more people should move to the city center but who doesn't realize this will cause more buildings to be built. That person believes something but doesn't believe a natural implication of their idea.

D. Marcuse says that *corporations* benefit from advertising (lines 13-15). Marcuse doesn't mention totalitarian political systems or whether they benefit from advertising.

E. This isn't what Marcuse says at all. False needs don't become real needs. And advertising derives false needs from real needs (lines 17-21)....the passage never distinguishes real needs from "secondary real needs".
This answer is nonsense designed to sound plausible because it uses some words that appeared in the passage.

Question 20

DISCUSSION: When a question quotes lines, you should always read around them. If you read lines 31-34, the term "forces of persuasion" is clear.

It's the manipulations of advertisers. The argument in paragraph 3 says that these manipulations change even our instinctive judgements (line 34).

A. The passage isn't about "dishonest" claims in advertising. Misinformation is only mentioned in passing in line 40.

B. If you read lines 31-34, line 32 is clearly referring to advertisers. Advertisers are not innate and instinctive drives.

C. This answer aims to confuse you by making up a term similar to one that was mentioned elsewhere in the passage ("emotional").
The passage never mentions "emotional pressure". Line 44 mentions emotional fulfillment. That has nothing to do with line 32.

D. "Social indoctrination" *might* refer to advertising (it's a stretch), but the passage definitely doesn't talk about state sponsored indoctrination.
This answer only makes sense if you're trying to prove it right, and paper over the flaws. Instead, you should be trying to prove answers wrong.

E. CORRECT. If you read all of lines 31-34, they say exactly this. Line 31 says "manipulation of advertisers". Line 34 says that this manipulation, these forces of persuasion affect our instinctive judgements.

Question 21

DISCUSSION: The passage ends with the author's critique of Marcuse. The author thinks consumers are able to respond consciously and rationally to ads.

The author has *not* said that ads are good. Instead, they are only arguing that Marcuse's critique isn't a good critique.

A. CORRECT. This matches the author's opinion. The author hasn't said that advertising is a good thing. Instead, their point is that Marcuse's critique is not a good one.

B. Nonsense. The entire fourth paragraph criticizes Marcuse. The author doesn't think Marcuse's claims are justified. And politics plays no part in this passage.

C. The passage doesn't talk about corporate leaders. Presumably, they have some responsibility for ordering ads, but it would be odd to end the passage by focussing on people who had never been mentioned before.

D. The author never talks about benefits of advertising. This answer has no support.

E. Marcuse *didn't* claim that "few people" are unable or unwilling to distinguish real from false needs. Marcuse claimed that *all of us* are subject to false needs.

Passage 4 – Property Justice
Questions 23–27

Paragraph Summaries

Passage A

1. Justice in acquisition describes how to own something that wasn't owned before. Justice in transfer describes how to transfer property.
2. We can use those principles to create an exhaustive theory of just property ownership.
3. A principle of rectification is required to deal with past injustices, such as theft.

Passage B

1. The Indian Nonintercourse Act protects Native American land from fraudulent transfers.
2. As a separate issue, there's a certain way of reasoning about Native American land claims: Natives were the original owners and land should be returned to them where possible.

Analysis

The first passage is very abstract. It describes a theory for the just ownership of property. So Passage A is merely describing a set of moral principles. They aren't the laws of any country. Instead, the principles can be used to judge if the laws of a country are just.

There are three cases to be covered:

1. Acquiring new property. If you find a rock that no one owns and you want to keep it as your property, how can you do that justly?
2. Transfer of property. If you want to justly transfer ownership of the rock to a new owner, how can you do that?
3. If someone steals the rock, and it ends up in a pawn shop, how can the injustice be corrected?

Note that the passage is *not* saying precisely how these goals can be achieved. The author doesn't tell us what's required for just ownership or transfer or property.

Instead, they're saying that if we can create principles to cover these three situations, we'll have a complete theory of property justice.

Passage B is more concrete. It's in two parts. The first part describes the history and purpose of the Indian Nonintercourse Act.

The purpose of the law is to prevent fraudulent transfers. Probably in the early years, American settlers tried to fool Native Americans out of their lands. After all, the American property system was foreign to Native American conceptions of property, and it would have been easy to make Natives "sell" their land without their realizing they had in fact entirely lost ownership of their land.

The second paragraph of passage B is actually on a completely different topic. It's no longer talking about the Indian Nonintercourse Act. Instead, paragraph 2 is a general discussion of native land claims in general.

Paragraph 2 says that *all* land in North America was illicitly taken from Native Americans. In a perfect world, it all ought to be transferred back to them.

That's not likely to happen, but it's still a worthy goal, according to this theory. This is a specific application of the principle of rectification described in passage A.

So to sum up, passage B has two different themes:

1. The Indian Nonintercourse Act, which restricts how land owned by Natives may be bought.
2. A line of argument (which the author may not agree with) that describes how to deal with land previously owned by Natives. In theory we ought to give *all* of it back, and even in practice we should give as much back as we can.

Question 22

DISCUSSION: Passage A was written to describe how we can make a theory of justice for property and what it might look like.

Passage B discusses a specific law that aims to prevent injustice in Native American land sales. Then passage B discusses native american land claims in the context of the principle of rectification.

In practice, you should eliminate answers if one of the passage descriptions is wrong.

A. Passage B doesn't criticize solutions.
B. **CORRECT.** This works. Passage A is an overview of how to make a just law for property. Passage B discusses two different aspects of justice in Native American land ownership issues.
C. Passage A *doesn't* give any details. It's an abstract discussion of moral principles. You couldn't use passage A to make detailed laws.
D. Passage B doesn't criticize any moral theory.
E. Passage B doesn't provide any counterexamples to a moral theory.

Question 23

DISCUSSION: The best way to answer this type of question is to eliminate answers you're sure don't appear in one of the passages. But be careful....use a high standard of certainty.

For instance, I knew that passage A is entirely concerned with theory, and not practice. This eliminated B, C and D. Often, awareness of the main idea of a passage can show what it wouldn't mention.

A. **CORRECT.** See lines 15-18 and lines 36-39. Passage B is the one that requires explanation. It's true that the transfers in lines 36-39 require federal approval, but they're still transfers from one owner to another.
B. Passage A doesn't mention any legal basis for anything. Passage A is an abstract moral discussion that doesn't descend to the level of specific laws.
C. Only passage A discusses the possibility of property rights in a wholly just world (lines 9-10). Passage B say "ideally" on line 56, but that's just an aside. Passage B isn't concerned with describing an ideal world and property rights in that world.
D. Passage A is concerned with theory. It talks about rectification, but it does not pay attention to whether its theory is practical or not.
E. Only passage B mentions an invasion (line 53).

Question 24

DISCUSSION: The second paragraph of passage B discusses how we can justly deal with Native American claims to land that was taken from them.

This relates to the final paragraph of passage A. That paragraph discussed how we can fix past illegal transfer of property. Passage A called this the principle of rectification.

A. Passage B isn't developing theory. Instead, passage B is talking about what we could do *in practice* to prevent injustice to Native Americans and to fix past injustices committed against Native Americans.
B. The second paragraph of passage B isn't trying to support a theory with facts.
C. The two texts are not structurally parallel. Passage A is entirely theoretical, while passage B is practical.
D. **CORRECT.** The second paragraph of passage B argues that we should fix past theft of Native American property. Passage A describes the moral theory behind fixing injustices.
E. Ridiculous. Passage A described a theory that recommended fixing past injustices. And the second paragraph of passage B describes a specific case where injustice should be fixed.

Question 25

DISCUSSION: Passage A is pure theory and moral idea. Passage B is the application of those moral ideas to a specific case.

The two passages are complementary; the author of passage B likes the ideas in passage A. Three wrong answers present titles that disagree with each other. So these answers can be eliminated instantly.

A. These titles are opposed to each other. Passages A and B were in general agreement.
B. Same as A.
C. These two topics are complete different....fruit trees, and cooking? Passage A and B were both on the subject of property.
D. Same as A.
E. **CORRECT.** This matches. The first title is a theoretical overview of the subject. The second title is a practical application.

Question 26

DISCUSSION: I originally got this question wrong because I didn't read carefully. The Indian Nonintercourse Act is only about the transfer of property currently owned by Natives.

The Nonintercourse act is *not* about restoring Native land that was unjustly taken. That's a completely different topic, that was discussed in the second paragraph of passage B. Paragraph 2 of Passage B is a theoretical discussion. It has nothing to do with the Nonintercourse act.

A. The purpose of the Nonintercourse Act is the just *transfer* of property. It has nothing to do with legitimizing existing holdings.
For instance, if land had been improperly seized in 1785 (before the act) the act could not apply to that seizure. The law only covers current transfers.

B. The Nonintercourse Act was a *new* law. It didn't clarify existing laws....it added to them.

C. Justice in acquisition is in lines 12-14. It covers acquisition of property *that no one owns yet.* The Indian Nonintercourse Act deals with land *already owned* by Natives.

D. CORRECT. Lines 41-44 pretty much say this directly. The law governs transfer of Native lands, and the intent is to make sure transfers are just.

E. I chose this answer. Paragraph *two* of passage B is about rectification of past injustices. But the Nonintercourse Act is only intended to prevent *new* injustices from occurring during land transfers.

Question 27

DISCUSSION: Passage A is entirely theoretical. Passage B is practical. The two passages agree with each other, but they're discussing different aspects of the issue.

The right answer focusses on a subtle aspect of passage B. The second paragraph of passage B is not necessarily the author's opinion. Instead, the author is merely sketching out a method of reasoning.

This is common in arguments. Authors will describe an argument without necessarily endorsing it. This allows the author to then discuss aspects of the argument or disagree with the argument.

A. CORRECT. Passage A is entirely theoretical. The first part of this answer is clear.
You might have hesitated about the description of passage B. But look at lines 48-50....the author says "one natural way of reasoning....is this". The author isn't saying that's *their* way of reasoning. They might not agree with it. A central feature of arguments is being able to make an argument you don't agree with in order to discuss or disagree with that argument.

B. Passage A never mentions any competing views of property. They talk as if they're describing the only possible just theory of property.

C. Passage A makes no policy recommendations. Policy recommendations are practical, but passage A is entirely theoretical.

D. Passage A doesn't briefly state a view. Passage A's view is the entire passage. And passage A doesn't provide an argument to justify their view. We're just supposed to take their word that this is a good theory of property. The author writes as if they're obviously describing the only valid principles of property.

E. Passage B doesn't attempt to undermine any views. The author presents a view in the second paragraph, but they don't agree or disagree with that view.

Section II – Logical Reasoning

Question 1

QUESTION TYPE: Necessary Assumption

CONCLUSION: 60% of the contractor's technicians are unqualified.

REASONING: 60% of the contractor's technicians are not certified by the Heating Technicians Association.

ANALYSIS: This argument is assuming that only those who are certified are qualified.

On necessary assumption questions the flaw is often obvious if you isolate the conclusion and reasoning. There's usually a difference in terms.

A. Pay doesn't matter. The argument didn't even mention pay.
Negation: Certified technicians do not receive higher pay than uncertified technicians.

B. It doesn't matter if some other contractors are worse than the one the city chose. It only matter if some other contractors are better.
Negation: One contractor in Ecuador has 39% of technicians certified. All other contractors in the world have 40% certified.

C. **CORRECT.** This exposes the flaw in the argument. The author didn't make a link between certification and qualification.
Negation: Technicians can be qualified even if they're not certified.

D. It doesn't matter who installed the systems in the past. We're talking about the *current* technicians and whether they are qualified.
Negation: The heating system was installed by trained monkeys.

E. It doesn't matter if there's a potential conflict of interest. The question was *only* talking about whether the technicians are qualified.
Negation: The contractor has no personal ties to city officials.

Question 2

QUESTION TYPE: Paradox

PARADOX: When salespeople say "thank you" after a sale, people say "thank you" back to them. When friends say thank you for a favor, people reply with "you're welcome".

ANALYSIS: You're looking for something that explains *the difference* in responses. None of the wrong answers show a difference between the two situations.

A. This answer makes the situation *more* confusing. If you think you're doing someone a favor, you normally say "you're welcome", not "thank you".

B. This just tells us that customers are free to say anything. This doesn't explain *why* customers say thank you.

C. This is a fact about *salespeople*. We're looking for something that tells us why *customers* say "thank you".

D. This doesn't explain why people respond differently when salespeople say "thank you" vs. when friends say "thank you".

E. **CORRECT.** This explains things by providing a difference between the two situations. If you feel you're doing a favor, you'll say "you're welcome", but if you feel you're getting a benefit, you're more likely to say "thanks".

That's just common sense, by the way. You know from outside knowledge how people respond when they're thanked for a favor, and how they respond when they've been given a benefit. This answer allows and requires you to apply that knowledge.

Question 3

QUESTION TYPE: Flawed Reasoning

CONCLUSION: It's rarely a good idea for video game makers to sell the movie rights to their games.

REASONING: One time, when a company sold movie rights to a game, things ended badly.

ANALYSIS: This is a very weak argument. The story about StarQuanta and *Nostroma* sounds persuasive, because *Nostroma* was a best-selling game.

But it's still just *one* example. A single example can't prove that it's always a bad idea to sell movie rights.

A. CORRECT. To draw a general conclusion you should have more than one example.

B. This contradicts the stimulus. The argument clearly said that the movie was hated "by critics and the public alike".
Also, this is nonsense. The stimulus *never* predicted that a product would be hated. They said that a product (the movie) *was* hated. That's not a prediction.
Example of flaw: The critics don't like this video game. Therefore, the public will hate it.

C. This answer means "circular reasoning". That didn't happen here. Circular reasoning is very rare.
Example of flaw: Selling movie rights is a bad idea because it's never a good idea to sell movie rights.

D. I have no idea what this answer refers to.
Example of flaw: This movie with lots of sex scenes was popular. Therefore, this video game with lots of sex scenes will be popular.

E. This refers to mixing up sufficient and necessary conditions. That didn't happen.
Example of flaw: Good video games must be challenging. This game is challenging, therefore it's good.

Question 4

QUESTION TYPE: Principle

PRINCIPLE:

Consultant has business interests AND executive salary determined by consultant → executive likely overpaid

ANALYSIS: The principle is very simple, once you reduce it to conditional form. We have one set of sufficient conditions, which let us conclude the necessary condition: the executive is likely overpaid.

We can *only* conclude necessary conditions. You can also prove the necessary condition of the contrapositive:

Executive not likely overpaid → salary not determined by consultant OR consultant had no business interests

You can never prove sufficient conditions. So it's never possible to prove, for example, that an executive is paid fairly, since that's not the necessary condition of this principle.

This realization about what you can and can't prove usually lets you eliminate all but 1-2 answers on this type of principle question. Focus on necessary conditions, and you can do this type of question much faster. In this case, only B and D are possible answers, because they're the only ones that conclude the necessary condition.

A. The principle does *not* let us conclude that an executive is definitely overpaid. This answer starts out wrong.

B. This answer starts off right. But it doesn't mention consultants. The sufficient condition of the principle was that salary was determined by a consultant with business interests with the company.

C. We *can't* conclude "probably not overpaid". We can only conclude the necessary condition of the principle, which was "probably overpaid".

D. CORRECT. This follows the principle exactly.

E. We can't conclude "not overpaid". We can only conclude the necessary condition of the principle: "probably overpaid".

Question 5

QUESTION TYPE: Flawed Reasoning

CONCLUSION: Lemaitre's theory is not correct.

REASONING: Both Lemaitre's theory and another theory are consistent with observations.

ANALYSIS: I'll give an example. Suppose I say "I think the box is full of lead" and someone else says "I think the box is full of iron".

We pick up the box. It's heavy. That's consistent with both theories. Either theory could be right, so it's wrong to say "the box can't be full of lead because a competing theory is consistent with the facts". Both theories have an equal amount of support, so they can't be used as evidence against each other.

A. The argument doesn't talk about the person behind the other theory. Their expertise isn't relevant. The only thing that matters is that their theory is also consistent with observation.

B. What term? And how did it shift in meaning? You need to be very precise to pick this sort of answer. I don't see that any term shifted.

C. The author didn't assume causation.
Example of flaw: The light went off, and there was a noise. Therefore, the light caused the noise.

D. CORRECT. Both theories predicted the data. Since they both have equal support, we can't use Lemaitre's theory to prove the other theory wrong. It could also be the case that the other theory is right and Lemaitre's is wrong.

E. The author didn't say that only the two theories in question could be right. They just said Lemaitre's wasn't right.
Example of flaw: Both theories could be right. Therefore, they're the only possible theories.

Question 6

QUESTION TYPE: Principle – Strengthen

CONCLUSION: It is wrong to criticize *Quirks* for not being realistic.

REASONING: *Quirks* is funny. And the important thing for a comedy is for it to be funny.

ANALYSIS: This already sounds like a pretty good argument. We can strengthen it by showing that a comedy film shouldn't be criticized as long as it succeeds as a comedy.

A. This *weakens* the argument. *Quirks* is not realistic.

B. This answer is tempting. It's true that *Quirks* was popular. But you're trying to strengthen the reasoning of the argument, and the author wasn't arguing that *Quirks* is good because it's popular. Instead, the author argued that *Quirks* is good because it's funny.

C. As with B, this doesn't strengthen the author's reasoning. Their point was that *Quirks* was good because it is funny. The fact that the characters are stylized would actually be a *bad* thing except for the fact that the film is funny.

D. CORRECT. This works. *Quirks* is a comedy, and it was funny. Being funny is what's important for a comedy.
This answer tells us that *Quirks* was successful overall, because it was a success as a comedy. And if *Quirks* was successful, then presumably it shouldn't be criticized for being unrealistic.

E. This doesn't help. We don't even know if *Quirks* tried to stay within a single genre. Moreover, this answer doesn't help prove that we shouldn't criticize *Quirks*.

Question 7

QUESTION TYPE: Flawed Parallel Reasoning

CONCLUSION: It is wrong to say that Party X did something illegal.

REASONING: Party Y accused Party X of illegal activity. Party Y once did something illegal.

ANALYSIS: This argument makes an ad hominem flaw. The author assumes that Party Y's argument is wrong just because Party Y once did something illegal.

Party Y could be right, even though they've previously done illegal things.

A. This is a bad argument, but it's not an ad hominem flaw.
The flaw here is that while it may or may not be immoral to break the law in question, it's certainly illegal.

B. This is actually a good argument. If you break a law and then accuse someone of the same violation, you *are* a hypocrite.
In the stimulus, the author did not accuse Party Y of hypocrisy. They accused them of being wrong. That's a different accusation.

C. **CORRECT.** This matches the structure. It says the plaintiff is *wrong* in their accusation because they also did the same thing.
But it's possible the plaintiff's accusation is right, even if the plaintiff is also guilty of the same violation.

D. This is a bad argument, but it's not an ad hominem flaw.
The error here is that the accusations could be correct even if they were only made to stir up controversy.

E. This is a bad argument, but it's not an ad hominem flaw.
The plaintiff only said that the defendant will benefit from the laws they vote for. That's either true or it's not. It doesn't matter whether the votes were justifiable. That's a separate question from whether the votes benefitted the defendant.

Question 8

QUESTION TYPE: Necessary Assumption

CONCLUSION: Eyes are only adapted to an animal's needs.

REASONING: The box jellyfish has eyes with powerful lenses, but can't use them due to poor retinas. This only lets box jellyfish see the prominent features but not the fine detail of objects.

ANALYSIS: On necessary assumption questions, you should look for a shift in terms, or a concept used in the conclusion that wasn't used in the argument.

The conclusion talks about eyes being adapted to needs. Yet the argument doesn't tell us what a box jellyfish needs. Maybe box jellyfish actually do need eyes that can focus on fine detail!

A. It doesn't matter what other jellyfish can do.
Negation: One other type of jellyfish can't focus clearly.

B. **CORRECT.** The conclusion talked about needs, but the argument never said what a box jellyfish needs! This answer bridges that gap.
Negation: Box jellyfish need to detect the fine details of objects.

C. This assumption would *weaken* the argument.
The author was implying that box jellyfish didn't need better vision, which explains their oddly useful yet useless eyes.
Note: The negation of this answer appears to strengthen the argument. But negations are supposed to *destroy* the argument, not strengthen it!
Negation: Box jellyfish wouldn't benefit from better vision.

D. This answer just makes the situation confusing.
If the ancestor jellyfish used to have better eyes, then why did the box jellyfish lose this ability?
There's a difference between not developing a better feature and intentionally losing a better feature because you don't need it.

E. It doesn't matter if box jellyfish have other means of detection. The core of this argument is whether box jellyfish *need* better vision, for whatever reason.

Question 9

QUESTION TYPE: Weaken

CONCLUSION: The evidence helps show that advertising does in fact influence smoking.

REASONING: Countries with smoking advertising restrictions have had great reductions in first time smoking.

ANALYSIS: This feels like a good argument, because we already tend to think tobacco advertising is bad. But actually, the author has just shown a correlation between smoking advertising restrictions and reductions in first time smoking.

Whenever there's a correlation, there are four possibilities:

1. Restrictions reduce first time smoking.
2. Reduced first time smoking causes restrictions.
3. Some third factor causes both reduced first time smoking and advertising restrictions.
4. The correlation is random.

You can weaken the correlation by showing that one of the other four possibilities exists.

A. This doesn't address the issue. The stimulus was talking about a reduction in *first time smokers*. People who already smoke are a different group.
B. This is an irrelevant fact about the nature of the advertising restrictions. We care about the *effect* of the restrictions, not the legal fine print.
C. **CORRECT.** This is number three from the list above. If this is true, then it's possible a third factor (negative attitudes towards smoking) are the cause of both the advertising restrictions and the reduction in first time smoking.
D. The stimulus was only talking about the number of first time smokers. It doesn't matter what happens after people start.
This answer also says nothing about whether advertising changes attitudes.
E. This is an irrelevant fact about advertising. For this to matter, we'd need to know *what percentage* of people are relatively unaffected by tobacco advertising. And other advertising doesn't matter.

Question 10

QUESTION TYPE: Sufficient Assumption

CONCLUSION: Bertolt Brecht's plays are not successful dramas.

Brecht play → ~~successful~~

REASONING: In successful plays, audiences must care what happens to at least some characters. In Brecht's plays, it's hard to figure out anyone's personality.

Brecht play → ~~personality~~
successful → care

ANALYSIS: Sufficient assumption questions are very formulaic. Start by taking the conclusion, and splitting it far apart.

Brecht play ~~successful~~

Then, attach the reasoning onto these terms. I've taken the contrapositive of one to do so (~~care~~ → ~~successful~~)

Brecht play → ~~personality~~ ~~care~~ → ~~successful~~

You can probably see the gap. To prove this argument correct, we have to show that if audiences can't figure out personalities, then they won't care about characters.

A. CORRECT. This matches the gap in the diagram above.

B. This just strings together two concepts that were in a single premise. These words are found in the second sentence.
The more you see a word or idea, the more you like it – it's a known psychological bias. Watch out for answers that merely reuse words that were in the stimulus.

C. The LSAT uses "directly proportional" in wrong answers fairly frequently. Directly proportional means: if one thing goes up 10%, then another thing also goes up by exactly 10%.
Direct proportionality is almost *never* relevant in an argument. Do you care if your LSAT score is *directly* proportional to law school application success?

D. Notice that the second sentence *already* says that both audiences and actors can't understand Brecht's personalities. This answer just adds an irrelevant rule that would only affect plays other than Brecht's.

E. "Personality → succeed" is what this answer says. This doesn't help us prove what plays *don't* succeed. To prove that, you need "not succeed" to be a necessary condition.

Question 11

QUESTION TYPE: Identify the conclusion

CONCLUSION: There's no harm in accepting the gift of high tech streetlights.

REASONING: Competitive bidding prevents gifts from influencing city contract bids. And the gift's only ulterior motive is publicity during an upcoming convention. (The lights will be seen by mayors of *other* cities)

ANALYSIS: The word "surely" is significant. Anytime someone says "surely" they are indicating their opinion. Ironically, "surely" indicates the author is not sure.

Any statement of opinion, of uncertainty, is usually the author's conclusion. So this argument's conclusion is that there's no harm to accepting the gifts.

Another way of looking at it is to ask: why are they telling me this? In this case, the argument is about whether to accept the gift. The author concludes "why not? There's no harm". All of the evidence is aimed at showing this lack of harm (competitive process prevents corruption, only ulterior motive is aimed at other cities)

A. The author didn't say this. The company might very well want to influence bidding. What the author *did* say is that competitive bidding prevents influence.

B. CORRECT. See the analysis above.

C. This *contradicts* the stimulus. The author said there's no harm in allowing the gift.

D. This is a fact that supports the conclusion. The conclusion is that therefore there's no harm to accepting the gift.

E. This is a fact supporting the conclusion. Since the motive of the gift is not aimed at the city, then there's no harm in accepting the gift.

Question 12

QUESTION TYPE: Sufficient Assumption

CONCLUSION: The chairperson shouldn't have released the report.

REASONING: The chairperson didn't ask any other committee members whether the report should be released.

ANALYSIS: On sufficient assumption questions, you should look for a gap between reasoning and conclusion.

Here, we know only one fact: the members weren't asked. We need to connect this to the conclusion. To prove that release was wrong, we should say "if members weren't asked, then release was wrong". The right answer is worded a bit differently (it's harder to understand!) but it has the same effect.

Normally, you can diagram sufficient assumption questions. That's because there are multiple conditional statements to link together. But this question doesn't even *have* a conditional statement to diagram. There are just two separate facts. Diagramming is a useful tool, but don't try to apply it blindly where it has no use.

A. CORRECT. The contrapositive of this is:
"~~consent~~ → ~~permissible~~"
Since the chairperson didn't ask the members, we don't know whether they consented
Therefore, the release was not permissible.

B. This *weakens* the argument. It doesn't prove that the release was ok, but this fact at least shows the members approved of the report.

C. We don't know whether any commission members had objections. This doesn't help.
Objection → ~~permissible~~

D. This doesn't work. It's possible that members would have agreed to a release if they had been consulted.
We need something that shows the release was wrong *because* the members weren't consulted.

E. This doesn't necessarily show the release was wrong. The stimulus never said that a release must obey the preferences of *all* members.

Question 13

QUESTION TYPE: Flawed Reasoning

CONCLUSION: Putting people in jail can't reduce crime.

REASONING: We put more people in jail, but the crime rate didn't decrease.

ANALYSIS: In this argument, the author ignores an obvious objection: would the crime rate still have stayed the same if we hadn't put people in jail?

It's possible that crime would have *risen* if fewer people were in prison. If that were true, then it's accurate to say that jail can reduce crime.

In other words, crime may naturally be increasing, but fortunately putting more people in jail has let us keep the crime rate stable.

A. The author didn't say this.
Example of flaw: The national crime rate increased. So our tiny town's reported crime rate must have increased, even though the only criminal retired.

B. CORRECT. It's possible that crime was rising, but jail time managed to keep the crime rate stable.

C. The *amount* of population doesn't matter. The crime *rate* is just the total amount of crimes divided by the population. Presumably, if population increases, then the number of crimes goes up as well. A certain percentage of every thousand people will be criminals.

D. The reformer didn't propose any alternate measures to reducing crime. Their conclusion was simply that jail doesn't work. It doesn't matter whether any other measures work.

E. I don't know what to say except that the argument didn't assume this.
Example of flaw: There were five crimes last year, and 3 prisoners. This year there were 10 crimes, double the number. So there must be 6 prisoners, double the number.

Question 14

QUESTION TYPE: Method of Reasoning

CONCLUSION: Winona says that it's silly to justify the space program due to its indirect research effects.

REASONING: We could just fund technology directly.

ANALYSIS: Ines justifies the space program due to its indirect technological spinoffs. Winona makes the argument that there's no need to fund space exploration, because we could just fund technology directly.

The answers are abstract. On a question like this, you should have an idea what you're looking for. Don't spend much time on any answer until you've looked at *all* of them. The right answer is often obvious once you get to it, so you don't want to waste 30 seconds on A or B before looking at D and E.

Rather than "explain" why the wrong answers are wrong, I've included examples of what each wrong answer would look like. There's no way to "explain" those answers because they simply aren't what Winona did.

A. Winona didn't say this.
Example of method: "You say the space program will have benefits. But there's no evidence that will happen."

B. Winona didn't say this.
Example of method: "You forgot that the space program causes terrible pollution from its use of fuel. This drawback outweighs the the program's research benefits."

C. Winona didn't say this.
Example of method: "You said the space program is inexpensive, and that massive investments in the program produced benefits. But if there have been massive investments, then the program was not inexpensive."

D. Winona didn't say this.
Example of method: "You say the space program will produce benefits. But that will cost 10 trillion dollars."

E. **CORRECT.** This is exactly what Winona does.

Question 15

QUESTION TYPE: Flawed Reasoning

CONCLUSION: The advertising campaign was bad.

REASONING: Sales were bad.

ANALYSIS: There are many factors that go into sales. Advertising is one, but product quality is also important, as is the economy, luck, competition, etc.

This is a causation-correlation error. The marketing consultant has shown a correlation between poor sales and the advertising campaign, but they haven't shown the campaign *caused* the low sales.

A. Very tempting answer. But think about what this actually means. If the ad campaign produced even a *single* sale, then sales would have been "lower still" in the absence of that campaign. The marketing consultant isn't arguing that the campaign was so useless that it failed to make even a single sale. Instead, they're arguing that campaign was not particularly effective.
Note: Competitor in this case refers to the competing consultant, I believe, though the sentence is ambiguous.
Example of flaw: Sales were poor after the new advertising campaign. So clearly, the advertising campaign didn't lead to a single sale.

B. **CORRECT.** There are multiple factors in any sale. Even the best advertising campaign might fail to produce sales if the economy is weak.

C. The author didn't say this.
Example of flaw: The new smartphone is new, so it will definitely sell better than all old smartphones.

D. The author didn't say this.
Example of flaw: The popular, established product sells better than this new, poorly manufactured product. The difference must be because of the effective advertising of the old product.

E. This describes a sufficient-necessary error. The argument didn't do this.
Example of flaw: To sell well, a product needs good advertising. This product has good advertising, so it will sell well.

Question 16

QUESTION TYPE: Method of Reasoning

CONCLUSION: We should award the architecture prize for the best building, rather than best architect.

REASONING: Architecture is like movies: buildings are made by teams, not individuals. We give awards for best picture.

ANALYSIS: This is an argument by analogy. There are two cases:

- Science, where Nobel prizes are awarded for individual work.
- Movie awards, which are given for the achievement itself. Movies are made by teams.

The argument says that architecture is similar to movies and unlike science.

A. CORRECT. This matches the stimulus. The author compares architecture to science and film. They say architecture is more like film, so we should give architecture awards like film awards.

B. What two objects?
Example of method: This diamond is rare, while this pez dispenser is common. So the diamond is more valuable.

C. The author didn't say there's a criticism that should be applied to two fields.
Example of method: It's wrong to cheat on the test because it gives you an unfair advantage. Using your family connections gives you an unfair advantage as well, so that's also wrong.

D. "Disanalogous" means different. The two different fields are science vs. architecture/film. This answer says that, because science is different, we can't use science to draw conclusions about architecture. Nonsense!
The author *used* science to make their argument. They say that because architecture is different from science, we shouldn't give architecture prizes like science prizes.

E. The argument didn't say that an action in a corresponding field is inappropriate.
The corresponding fields were: science and film. In each case, the author thought the action within that field was appropriate.

Question 17

QUESTION TYPE: Parallel Reasoning

CONCLUSION:
Most qualified elected AND Suarez not elected → Anderson elected

REASONING: Either Suarez or Anderson is the most qualified.

ANALYSIS: This is a good argument. There are only two candidates who could be most qualified: Suarez, or Anderson.

If the most qualified person is elected, it will be either Suarez or Anderson. So if the most qualified is elected and they *aren't* Suarez, they must be Anderson.

A. This answer doesn't say the lowest bidder is Caldwell or Qiu.

B. CORRECT. This matches the structure exactly. The lowest bidder is Dillon or Ramsey.
Lowest bidder chosen AND ~~Dillon~~ → Ramsey

C. This answer doesn't show that either Kapshaw or Johnson are the lowest bidder.

D. This answer sets up the wrong contrast. It should have said that either Holihan or Easton is the low bidder.
Instead, this answer says it's possible that they're both *not* low bidders.

E. The first part of this answer is right. It correctly shows that either Perez or Sullivan will be the lowest bidder.
But the second part doesn't match the structure. This argument should have concluded that if the contract went to the low bidder and Sullivan didn't get it, then Perez would.

Question 18

QUESTION TYPE: Flawed Reasoning

CONCLUSION: It is wrong to say that 15th century painters were better than 16th century painters.

REASONING: It's wrong to say that 15th century paintings were better because they were planimetric.

ANALYSIS: Suppose I make the following argument: "The moon is made of green cheese, therefore it's interesting."

That's a stupid argument. My evidence is wrong: the moon is not made of green cheese. But does that mean the moon is boring?

Of course not. A conclusion isn't false just because someone makes a bad argument.

The author showed the planimetric argument is not convincing. So the *argument for* the conclusion is wrong. But that doesn't mean the conclusion (15th century painters are better) is wrong.

A. This author didn't make an ad hominem flaw.
Example of flaw: An art historian argued that 15th century painters were better. But that art historian smells funny, so he's wrong.

B. To choose this kind of answer, you need to show two *clearly* different definitions of mastery.
Example of flaw: The painter has mastery over painting: he can paint very well. Therefore, he has mastery over all of painting: he controls the lives of all painters.

C. There was no sufficient-necessary error.
Example of flaw: If the argument were wrong, its author would hesitate. The author hesitates, so the argument is wrong.

D. A contradiction is two things that can't both be true. That didn't happen here.
Example of flaw: This painting is the best in the world, and almost as good as the one I own.

E. **CORRECT.** The position is: 15th century painters were better.
The author showed that the art historian's argument wasn't a good one. But a fact is not false just because a bad argument was made for that fact.

Question 19

QUESTION TYPE: Weaken

CONCLUSION: The object in the tomb was probably the head of a speaking staff, a communal object.

REASONING: Some say the object was mace, a type of weapon. But the object is too small to be a mace.

ANALYSIS: This is a question where the details matter. The speaking staff was a communal object, and it was found in a tomb.

The right answer uses both pieces of information. It says that communal objects were handed down across generations. That means they wouldn't likely be left in a tomb.

As a result of the way this question is structured, I wasn't able to prephrase anything. This is unusual – most modern LSAT questions can be predicted in advance. On this sort of question, where you can't predict, the key is to instead keep an open mind and be aware of all details.

A. It doesn't matter what other objects are in the tomb. But if there were no weapons, then that *strengthens* the argument. If there had been many weapons, then that might suggest that the object in question was also a weapon.

B. **CORRECT.** If an object is passed from generation to generation, then it won't be buried with someone in their tomb! This answer suggests the object in question was not a communal object and therefore not a speaking staff.

C. This sounds significant. But really, what does it prove? The fact that the object was rare doesn't help prove what it was.

D. A politically prominent person might be *more* likely to be buried with a significant object like a speaking staff. This certainly doesn't weaken the argument.

E. The fact that something *symbolizes* a weapon doesn't *make* it a weapon. If a speaking staff symbolizes a mace, it's still a speaking staff and not a mace.

Question 20

QUESTION TYPE: Necessary Assumption

CONCLUSION: To improve the soil, farmers must stop using chemical fertilizers.

REASONING: Farmers started using chemical fertilizers, and stopped growing green-manure crops such as alfalfa. This harmed farms' soil structure.

ANALYSIS: We're conditioned to think chemicals are bad. But the argument *didn't* say that chemical fertilizers hurt the soil. The argument said that the lack of alfalfa is what caused the poor soil structure.

Farmers might have stopped planting alfalfa because they thought they no longer needed it once they had fertilizer. But now that the damage is obvious, perhaps farmers could fix it by planting alfalfa again (without stopping fertilizer).

So the argument is assuming that farmers need to stop using chemical fertilizers before they can heal the soil with alfalfa.

A. The logic of this answer aside, negating a "most" statement is almost *never* significant. Moving from 51% to 50% is inconsequential in most situations apart from votes.
As for the logic of the answer: the argument is not assuming that if fertilizer goes away, the problem *will* be fixed (i.e. that lack of fertilizer is sufficient). Instead, the argument is assuming that lack of fertilizer is necessary.
Negation: Only half of the farmers who stop using chemical fertilizer will use alfalfa.

B. The point of the argument was that people stopped growing alfalfa entirely, after they began using chemical fertilizers. Farmers weren't applying fertilizers to alfalfa.

C. "The most important factor" is a reasonably common wrong answer. It almost never matters whether something is *the most* important factor. For instance, you know the LSAT is *an* important factor in law school admissions. Do you care whether it's *the most* important factor (rather than a close second, i.e. 51% vs. 49%)?

D. This would strengthen the argument, but it's not necessary. The point of the argument was that farmers stopped using alfalfa once they started using fertilizer. The lack of alfalfa is the real problem.

E. **CORRECT.** If many farmers may grow alfalfa again despite using chemical fertilizers, then it might not matter whether farmers still use chemicals.
Negation: Many farmers will grow green-manure crops even if they don't stop using chemical fertilizers.

Question 21

QUESTION TYPE: Must be True

FACTS:

1. Most Spanish 101 students attended every class.
2. Every student who scored lower than B-minus missed at least one class.

ANALYSIS: This is a mathematical question, and it tests how intuitively you understand the word "most". Let's say there were 9 students. "Most" of them would be five or more.

All the students who scored below B-minus missed every class. What's the largest number that could have done this? Four. That's because at least five students ("most") did attend every class.

This lets us conclude that at least five students scored b-minus or above. So "most" students scored b-minus and above.

Note the subtle differences in wording. It's easy to misread this question as saying that every student who scored b-minus or below missed a class. But the question doesn't say that....instead, it says every student who scored *below* b-minus missed class.

A. We don't know anything about students who scored A-minus or higher. Maybe only one student did that? (And the "most students" who attended classes all scored a B-plus)
B. This doesn't have to be true. It could be that only one student scored below b-minus, and 1,000 other students scored b-minus or above.
C. This is very tempting, and similar to E. Notice that the stimulus says every student who received a grade *below* a b-minus missed a class. That *doesn't* include students who scored exactly a b-minus. So this answer should have said "scored b-minus or higher".
D. This doesn't have to be true. Maybe all students who got b-minus or above attended every class. "most" can go as high as "all".
E. **CORRECT.** See the analysis for a full explanation. If most students attended all classes, then "most" students must have scored b-minus or above. Because no student who scored *below* b-minus had perfect attendance.

Question 22

QUESTION TYPE: Strengthen

CONCLUSION: Hypothesis: each separate sockeye salmon group adapted genetically to its habitat.

REASONING: The two groups of sockeye live in different parts of the lake and don't interbreed. The two groups also have genetic differences.

ANALYSIS: This is a difficult question; there's a lot of information to keep track of. Here are some alternative hypotheses:

- The genetic differences are just random genetic drift between populations that don't interbreed.
- One or both groups of sockeye bred with the native salmon, leading to genetic differences.

You can strengthen the answer by eliminating an alternate hypothesis.

You might wonder how I generated those hypotheses. Well, the LSAT expects you to have basic scientific knowledge, including an understanding of natural selection. If you know how natural selection works, those two hypotheses are the obvious alternate possibilities.

A. **CORRECT.** It's common scientific knowledge that interbreeding leads to genetic differences. So it's an alternate reason for genetic differences that doesn't involve adaptation. Eliminating a plausible alternative theory strengthens the researchers' hypothesis.
You're allowed, and expected, to use common scientific knowledge of facts to answer questions.
B. This doesn't tell us if the native salmon had different populations because they adapted to environments, or because of randomness.
C. This doesn't tell us anything about genetic differences.
D. This *weakens* the hypothesis. The hypothesis is that each population of sockeye adapted to its environment. If one sockeye has stayed the same genetically, then they likely *didn't* adapt.
E. The number of salmon doesn't matter. Adaptation to environment doesn't depend on total population numbers.

Question 23

QUESTION TYPE: Most Strongly Supported

FACTS:

1. Investment in modern technologies by businesspeople can increase growth in developing countries.
2. It's risky to be the first to invest.
3. If you succeed in your investment, people will copy you and eat up your profits.

ANALYSIS: There's an important distinction this question hints at but doesn't say directly: economies can grow even if entrepreneurs don't profit.

Suppose an entrepreneur invents a phone that can be controlled from your mind (cool!). Say it costs $500 to produce. Now imagine a 2nd entrepreneur copies the idea and sells the phone for exactly $500.

There's $0 profit for both entrepreneurs. But the economy has grown. We now have better phones! Most of the wrong answers ignore this difference between economic growth and individual profit.

A. This is silly. We know that the initial investment helps the economy. There's no evidence that further investment won't help the economy. We know that investment may not be profitable for entrepreneurs. But something can grow the economy even if entrepreneurs make no money.
B. There's no support for this. The argument doesn't say how much competition exists in traditional industries.
C. **CORRECT.** This is fairly well supported. There is currently little incentive for entrepreneurs to invest. But investment will probably increase economic growth. So if countries can encourage investment with incentives, they may see growth.
D. This isn't supported. The first sentence says that investment in modern industries is *one* way the economy can grow. But that doesn't mean its the *only* way to get growth.
E. This doesn't make sense. We know the first investment is risky. And we know the later investments eat up profit. And *nothing* says later investments are less risky. So it's quite possible that later investments are both risky and unprofitable.

Question 24

QUESTION TYPE: Paradox

PARADOX:

- People don't think the concert hall is a good concert hall.
- But they don't want to tear it down and replace it with a better one.

ANALYSIS: I couldn't prephrase this question. When that happens, just make sure you've clearly understood the paradox, then look for answers that explain it.

Most wrong answers will only address half of the paradox, if they address it at all. We need something that explains *both* facts.

A. This suggests the survey was biased in favor of replacement. If so, this makes the situation even more confusing: why didn't people decide to replace the concert hall?
B. This doesn't explain anything. It just confirms a fact we saw in the stimulus: people don't want the concert hall torn down. But that's still confusing, because people also don't think the concert hall is a good concert hall....
C. This explains why the construction industry might want the concert hall torn down. It doesn't explain why citizens agree the concert hall doesn't work yet don't want to tear it down.
D. **CORRECT.** This addresses the paradox. People *want* a new concert hall. And they do want to replace the existing hall. They just don't want to tear it down. Maybe the building is a nice building, and would work well for another purpose.
E. This makes the situation more confusing by adding a new advantage to tearing down the concert hall.

Question 25

QUESTION TYPE: Complete the Argument

CONCLUSION: The paper will be worse if the student can't find the book.

~~Book~~ → ~~Worse~~

REASONING: If they can't find the book, they can't make a citation, and therefore can't use the quotation. The paper will be worse without the quotation.

~~Book~~ → ~~Citation~~ → ~~Worse~~

ANALYSIS: To finish this, you need to look carefully at what the student says. They are not saying the paper will be ruined without the quotation. They're just saying the paper will be worse without the quotation.

The evidence already makes two conditional statements that can be connected. The conclusion just states the start and end of the conditional chain.

A. This doesn't follow. The student says they can't use the quotation without an *accurate* citation. So presumably there's no point to an inaccurate citation.

B. Look at the final sentence. The paper will be *better* with the quotation. That implies it's still possible to write the paper without the quotation. The paper will be worse, but it won't be impossible to finish.
Also, this answer leaves out "if I do not find the book".

C. **CORRECT.** This really fits well with the final sentence. The final sentence says the paper will be worse without the quote. And we know the book is necessary for the quote. So it follows that the book is necessary for not making the paper worse.

D. This contradicts the stimulus. The stimulus said that without the citation, the student can't include the quote.

E. Same as B. The student says their paper will be *worse* without the quotation. So presumably they still can finish the paper without it. The paper will just be lower quality.

Section III – Logic Games

Game – Five Instrumental Pieces

Questions 1–7

Setup

This is a pure sequencing game. Modern pure sequencing games are a *bit* different from traditional sequencing games, but not much. In the past, you could join all the rules together into one big diagram. But now, you usually have to draw the rules separately. Answering the questions quickly depends on your ability to retain these rules and apply them quickly.

You should aim to be very fast at these games, as they tend to be easy. I finished this one in five minutes on my first try. That leaves extra time for harder games.

Here are the three diagrams:

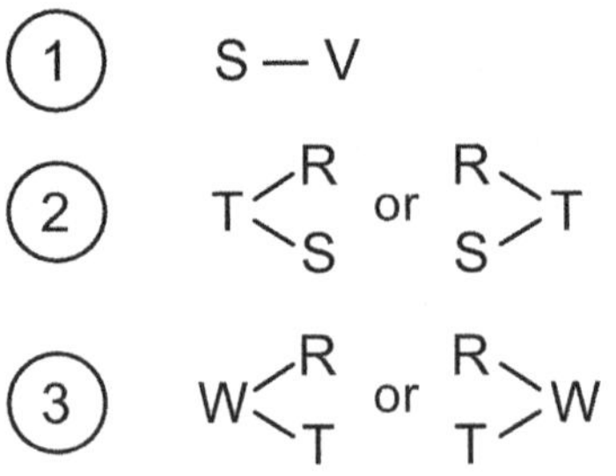

```
(1)   S — V

        R        R
(2)   T<    or     >T
        S        S

        R        R
(3)   W<    or     >W
        T        T
```

I didn't have any deductions beyond just drawing the rules. To answer the questions, I just quickly applied the rules to whatever situation the question presented.

The key is noticing that questions usually place a variable somewhere in a way that affects one of the rules. So each new rule on the questions allows deductions. Deductions lead to more deductions.

This is a step by step process that can and should be practiced. If you hesitate to apply rules, then you're not doing games as well as you can. Those who do best on games make deductions automatically, without thought.

Main Diagram

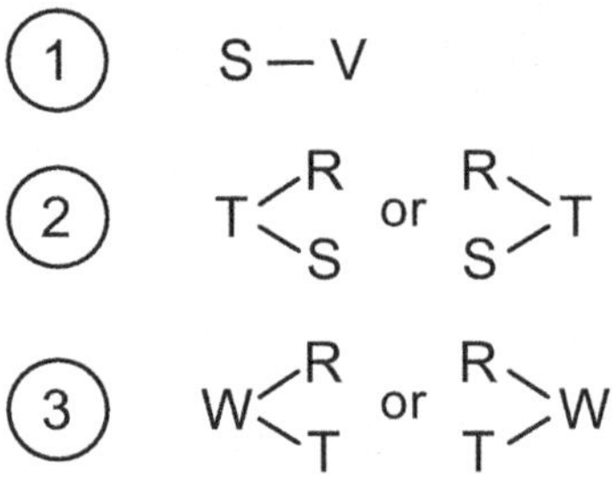

```
(1)   S — V

        R        R
(2)   T<    or     >T
        S        S

        R        R
(3)   W<    or     >W
        T        T
```


Question 1

For acceptable order questions, go through the rules and use them to eliminate answers one by one.

Rule 1 eliminates **D.** Salammbo has to be before Vancouver.

Rule 2 eliminates **A** and **E.** Trapezoid has to be before or after both Reciprocity and Vancouver.

Rule 3 eliminates **C.** Wisteria has to be before or after both Reciprocity and Trapezoid.

B is **CORRECT.** It violates no rules.

Question 2

This question places Salammbo fourth. Your first step should be to see which existing rule is affected by this, and draw it. Rule 1 says that Salammbo has to be earlier than Vancouver, so Vancouver goes last:

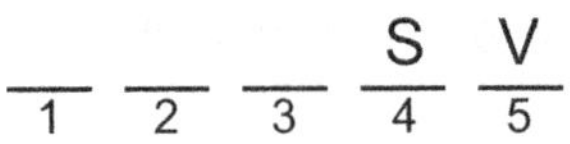

```
            S   V
__  __  __  __  __
1   2   3   4   5
```

Next, check which rules involve S or V. Rule 2 says that T has to be before both R and S, or after both R and S.

T *can't be* after S, since there's no space. That means that T is before S and before R. You can draw that on the diagram

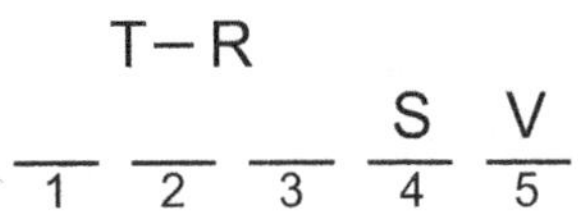

```
   T—R
            S   V
__  __  __  __  __
1   2   3   4   5
```

Note: the floating T-R is just a reminder that T – R exist, somewhere on the open spaces they're drawn floating above.

Once you make a deduction, check if that solves the question. It usually does. **C** is **CORRECT.**

Question 3

This question is good practice for making deductions. It places R first. This in turn leads to a massive chain of deductions that affects every variable. The deductions are about ordering, so I'm going to go step by step to create a sequencing diagram that applies to this question.

Let's go step by step. Rule 2 says that R + S are either both before or both after T. If R is first, then R + S must both before T:

S—T

Rule 1 says that V also comes after S:

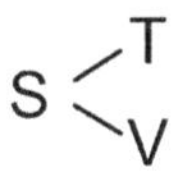

```
  /T
S
  \V
```

Rule 3 is affected too. W has to be before or after both R and T. Since R is first, then both R and T are before W. So we can add W after T on the diagram:

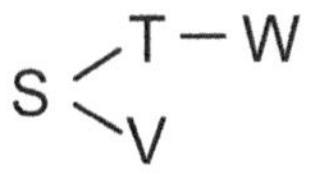

```
  /T—W
S
  \V
```

There are only four open spaces for these four variables. Since S has to be in front of all the other remaining variables, S has to be second.

We can draw the full diagram like this:

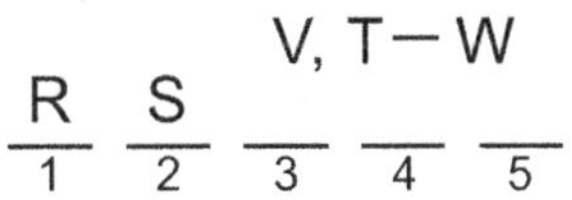

```
          V, T—W
R   S
__  __  __  __  __
1   2   3   4   5
```

This diagram shows us the rules that govern V, T and W. T is somewhere before W, and V could go anywhere.

You can use this framework to eliminate answers. The diagram above contradicts **A, C, D** and **E.**

B is **CORRECT.** This diagram proves that it's possible:

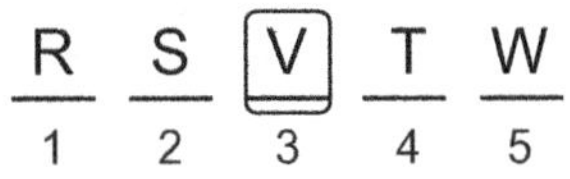

```
R   S  [V]  T   W
__  __  __  __  __
1   2   3   4   5
```

Question 4

Just like question 3, this question allows step by step deductions. This question places Trapezoid second, so hyou must think precisely about the rules involving T.

Rule 2 says that R and S must both be either before or after T. On this question, T is second, so there's only *one* space before T. Therefore, R and S must go after T.

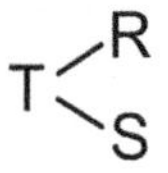

T < R, S

We also know that V is after S (rule 2). So there are a total of three people after T: R, and S – V.

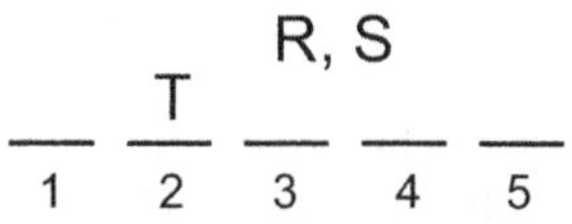

R, S

	T			
1	2	3	4	5

W is the only CD left to place, and first is the only spot open:

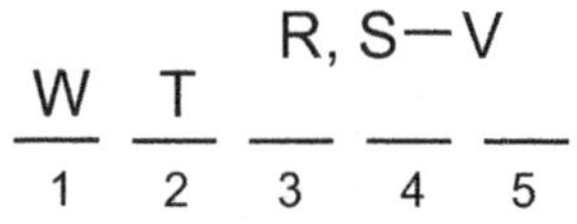

R, S—V

W	T			
1	2	3	4	5

You can use this diagram to eliminate answers.

A and **B** are wrong because W must go first.

C is wrong because V can go fourth at latest, since V is after S.

D is wrong because W must go first.

E is **CORRECT.** This diagram proves it:

W	T	S	V	R
1	2	3	4	5

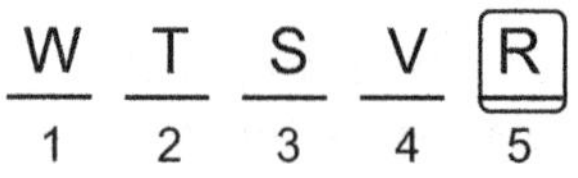

Question 5

At first, I thought this question would be very difficult. But each wrong answer is easy to eliminate if you use the rules. So take each rule and see what answers it eliminates.

Remember, the CDs in the answer choices refer to the first and second slots.

S needs to be before V (rule 1). So **A** is wrong.

The third rule proves **B** wrong. If W is after R, then W needs to be after both R *and* after T. In this answer W is only after R.

The second rule proves **C** wrong. T needs to be after both S *and* R. In this answer, T is only after S.

The third rule proves **D** wrong. W needs to be after T *and* R. In this answer, W is only after T.

I'll admit that **B, C** and **D** are a little hard to visualize. The key is knowing that on **B**, for example, R and W are mentioned in rule 3, and so is T. *Never let go of that idea.* If an answer (e.g. B) mentions both R and W, you also need to ask where T can go while obeying the rule. Look at rule 3 until you see how the answer violates it, because if it mentions variables from a rule it almost certainly violates that rule. Draw sketches if they help visualize.

A lot of people look at an answer, say "oh, **B** mentions things from rule 3, interesting", but then they let that thought drift out of their head. Always focus on the rules – if you make an observation, follow it till the end.

E is **CORRECT.** This diagram proves it is possible:

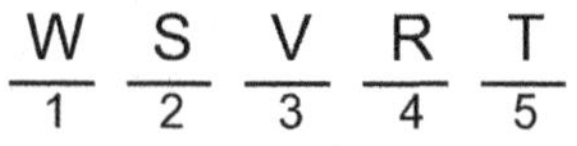

W	S	V	R	T
1	2	3	4	5

Question 6

Once again, this question gives us a new rule: V is second.

This affects rule 1. That rule says S is before V:

```
S   V
_   _   _   _   _
1   2   3   4   5
```

Don't stop there. S is also mentioned in rule 2: T has to be before or after both R and S.

Since S is first, that means T has to be after R and S:

```
            R—T
S   V
_   _   _   _   _
1   2   3   4   5
```

W could be anywhere, as long as it's before or after both R and T.

You can use the diagram above to eliminate all the wrong answers. **C** and **E** are the least obvious to eliminate. They're both wrong because they indirectly place T before R.

D is **CORRECT.** This diagram proves it.

```
S   V   W   R   T
_   _   _   _   _
1   2   3   4   5
```

Question 7

This question says that W is first. That actually doesn't lead to any new deductions. But it's still helpful to sketch all of the remaining variables:

```
        R, T, S—V
W
_   _   _   _   _
1   2   3   4   5
```

However, this diagram is a bit misleading. You also need to remember that T is either before both R and S, or after them. So really there are two possibilities. Either T is second:

```
          R, S
W   T           V
_   _   _   _   _
1   2   3   4   5
```

Or T is after R and S, and therefore, fourth or fifth. (I have no good diagram for this scenario).

In either case, T can't go third so **A** is **CORRECT.**

All of the other answers are possible. For practice, it is useful to try quickly sketching scenarios on your own that prove these answers are possible. If you think one of the other answers is impossible than you've likely misread or forgotten a rule.

Game 2 – Business Symposium
Questions 8–13

Setup

I don't know how to classify this game. It's not like any other I've seen. It has grouping and linear elements, but frankly, it's not useful to think of this game in those terms.

The main difficulty on this game is viewing the rules from the right perspective. Particularly the second rule. The second rule says something like this:

Xiao and Yoshida can't be before Zimmerman.

But actually, once you consider all the rules, this actually mean: Zimmerman must speak at 1pm. Once you figure that out, the game is easy. (Question 13 actually directly tests this deduction.)

I can't give you a magic bullet for finding this kind of deduction. The game is essentially testing your ability to visualize all five variables, and ask yourself who can go before Z (no one).

Rule 2 says that X and Y can't be before Z. And rule 1 says that M and L are in the same room.

So *only* M could go before Z. But if you did put M before Z, then one of X/Y would have to go first in the other room, like this:

G	X	Y	
R	M	Z	L
	1	2	3

This still violates rule 2. So we can conclude that Z *has* to go at 1pm.

The rest of the setup is just drawing these rules:

(1) [M—L] same

(2) Z=1pm

(3) $L_G \rightarrow Z_R — X_R$

Remember, anything that isn't forbidden is allowed. *Any* diagram is fine as long as it doesn't violate these rules.

Main Diagram

(1) [M—L] same

(2) Z=1pm

(3) $L_G \rightarrow Z_R — X_R$

Question 8

For acceptable order questions, go through the rules and use them to eliminate answers one by one.

Rule 1 eliminates **D** and **E.** Molina and Long have to be in the same room, and Molina has to be before Long.

Rule 2 eliminates **B.** Xiao can't be before Zimmerman.

Rule 3 eliminates **C.** If Long is in the gold room, then X must be in the Rose room.

A is **CORRECT.** It violates no rules.

Question 9

I skipped this question my first time through the game. I eventually came back and solved it by brute force. I drew diagrams disproving all the wrong answers.

This isn't the best approach, but it works perfectly fine if you have time for it. I did have time on this question since I finished the first game quite quickly.

The short way to solve this question is to have made the deduction that Zimmerman must go at 1pm.

If you know that, then it's obvious that **B** is **CORRECT.** This is because Long always go at 2pm or later (rule 1).

Here are diagrams proving the other answers are possible.

This diagram proves that **A** is possible:

G	M	L	
R	Z	Y	X
	1	2	3

This diagram proves that **C** is possible:

G	Y	M	L
R	Z	X	
	1	2	

This diagram proves that **D** is possible:

G	M	Y	L
R	Z	X	
	1	2	

This diagram proves that **E** is possible:

G	Y	M	L
R	Z	X	
	1	2	

You don't need to draw these brute force diagrams. I'm only drawing them in case you thought one of the wrong answers wasn't possible.

Question 10

If Xiao speaks at 3 pm, then there are three possibilities. They depend on where ML speak. The third rule says that if ML are in the Gold room, then X is in the Rose room:

```
G  M  L
R  Z  Y  X
   1  2  3
```

If ML are in the Rose room, then X could speak in either room. In both scenarios, ZY must be first in their room:

```
G  Z  Y  X
R  M  L
   1  2
```

```
G  Z  Y  X
R  M  L
   1  2
```

The three diagrams prove that **A** is **CORRECT.** Long can't be in the same room as Zimmerman in any scenario.

All of the other answers are possible in one or more diagrams.

Question 11

You can use the rules to eliminate answers.

Rule 1 eliminates **A** and **B.** M and L have to be in the same room, in that order.

Rule 2 eliminates **D.** Y can't be before Z.

Rule 3 eliminates **E.** If L is in the Gold room, then Z should be in the Rose room.

C is **CORRECT.** It violates no rules.

Question 12

This question places Y at 1 pm. We know from rule 2 that Z has to be first. (See the setup for a full explanation of that meaning of rule 2).

So Y and Z fill both 1pm slots. Their order doesn't matter. I've drawn Y in gold, but you could reverse Y and Z:

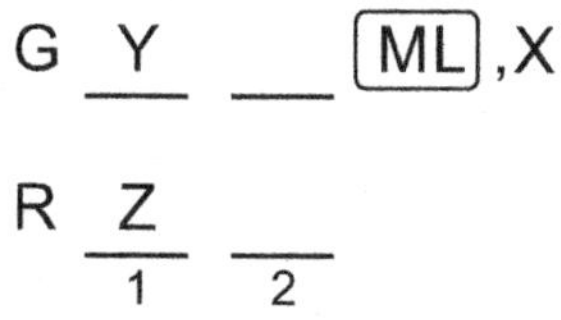

```
G  Y   __  [ML],X
R  Z   __
   1   2
```

ML and X are interchangeable between the Gold and Rose rooms in the above scenario. If ML goes in one room, X goes in the other.

The question is asking what could be true. It's possible to put ML with Y, so **C** is **CORRECT.**

None of the other answers are possible.

Question 13

I'll confess that I took a while to answer this question. When I first did the game, I hadn't realized that rule 2 meant that Z had to be in 1pm.

If you already made that deduction up front, the question is easy: **E** is **CORRECT.**

Otherwise, you can use process of elimination to eliminate the answers. There are two ways to eliminate an answer:

1. If it allows something that can't happen.
2. If it forbids something that normally can happen.

Many scenarios contradict **A.** Long doesn't have to be at 3pm. For example, this scenario is fine according to the normal rules:

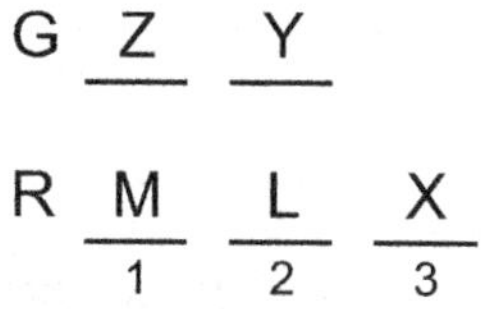

```
G  Z   Y
R  M   L   X
   1   2   3
```

B is true, but you're not just looking for an answer that is true. You're looking to replace the rule. **B** allows (wrong) scenarios like this:

```
G  X   Z
R  Y   M   L
   1   2   3
```

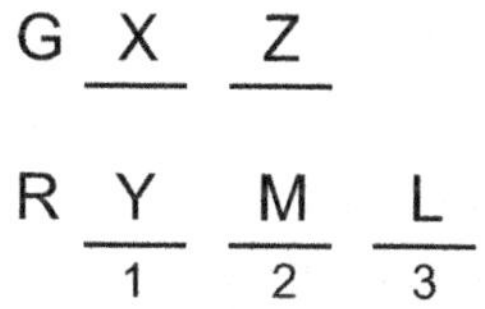

C is also true, but doesn't actually replace the rule. It allows wrong scenarios like this:

```
G  X   Z   Y
R  M   L
   1   2
```

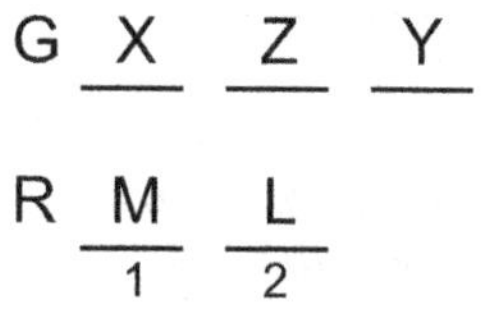

D is also something that must be true, but doesn't actually replace the rule. It allows wrong scenarios like this:

```
G  X   Y   Z
R  M   L
   1   2
```

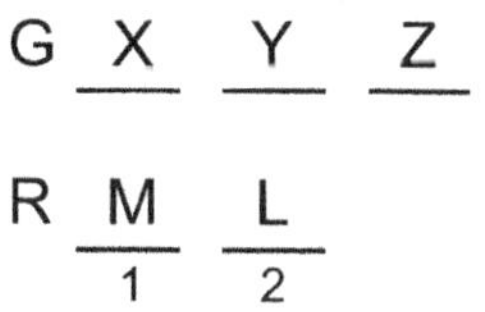

I'll expand on why **E** is **CORRECT.** The only speaker that can go before Z is M. But to place Z at 2pm we need *two* speakers to go before Z. That's because there are always two speakers at 1pm.

Since there aren't *two* speakers who can go before Z, we can't put Z at 2pm. Therefore Z always speaks at 1pm.

Game 3 – 17th Century Buildings
Questions 14–18

Setup

This is a grouping game. I set it up vertically, like the first question does:

T __

W __

Y __

The first rule is very important. It says that the Williamses owned more than the Yandells.

On the surface, you can't do much with that. But, you should always dig deep into rules to see their implications. There are five buildings. Be specific: how many could the Yandells own?

Not three. Then the Williamses could have two at most. The Yandells couldn't own two buildings, either. To have more, the Williamses would need three buildings. And that leaves none for the Trents (every family needs at least one building).

So the Yandells can only have one building, and the Williamses need at least two. You can draw this on the diagram:

T __

W __ __

Y __ |

This may seem like a small deduction, but it makes the game *far* easier.

The other two rules I couldn't place on the diagram. I just drew them, and made sure I memorized them. Going fast depends on your ability to memorize the rules and know them automatically:

(1) F ←|→ I, M

(2) T_S or Y_I

Note that in the second rule, I know that the "or" is an inclusive or: both are possible. Some details I simply commit to memory if there's no good way to draw them.

There's nothing else to say about the setup. Speed depends on applying these rules quickly.

Main Diagram

T __

W __ __

Y __ |

(1) F ←|→ I, M

(2) T_S or Y_I

Question 14

For acceptable order questions, go through the rules and use them to eliminate answers one by one.

Rule 1 eliminates **D** and **E.** The Williamses need to own more buildings than the Yandells.

Rule 2 eliminates **C.** The forge and the mill can't have the same owner.

Rule 3 eliminates **B.** Either the Trents own the stable or the Yandells own the inn.

A is **CORRECT.** It violates no rules.

Question 15

At first glance, this question was difficult. There's no obvious way to eliminate answers. It feels like you must use brute force.

But there is *always* a short way. The trick is to look at what rules affect the Trents. Only the final rule:

- Trents need stables, OR Yandells need the inn.

Next, think of the answers in terms of "easy" and "hard". Does the answer make it easier to fulfill the rule, or harder? Easy and neutral answers are unlikely candidates to be correct, whereas hard answers are usually correct.

Easy answers give the Trents the stable. They help fulfill the rule.

Neutral answers don't give the Trents the stable, but leave the inn alone. They don't affect the rule.

Hard answers don't give the Trents the stable, and they do give the Trents the inn. This contradicts the rule.

D is **CORRECT.** If the Trents have the inn, then the Yandells don't have it. So this answer violates rule 3.

I'll explain my approach from a different perspective. I knew that rule three was important, since the question mentions the Trents. I knew that rule three mentioned S and I. So I looked for answers that affected those variables. **D** was the likely candidate, since it mentioned I, and also *didn't* give the Trents S.

This is a bit hard to explain since it's an intuitive process, but basically you want to approach the answers from the perspective of the rule and whether the answer helps or hurts the odds of fulfilling the rule. Then once you identify a good candidate you can examine it more closely.

Question 16

This question gives you a new rule: the Yandells owned the mill. You should draw that:

T __

W __ __

Y M |

The Yandells can only have one building, because the Williameses need more buildings than the Yandells (see the setup for a full explanation). So only two groups are left.

Consider how this affects the existing rules. M was in rule 2. The rule in full was that F can't go with I or M.

F and I are left, and they can't go together. Only two groups are left. So one of F and I goes in each group:

T F/I __

W I/F __

Y M |

This type of deduction comes from focussing on one rule at a time, and thinking through the implications.

Now let's look at the remaining rules. Rule 3 says that the Yandells need the inn or the Trents need the stable. Since the Yandells can't take more buildings, we need to give the Trents the stable:

T F/I S

W I/F __

Y M |

Finally, the Williamses need another building so that they have more buildings than the Yandells. Therefore, we need to give them the granary:

T F/I S

W I/F G

Y M |

Usually, the final deduction is the right answer, and that's true on this question. **D** is **CORRECT.**

Question 17

This question says one family owned the granary and the inn. You should ask: who can do that. The Yandells can't, because they can only have one building.

So it's got to be the Trents or the Williamses. Let's try the Trents:

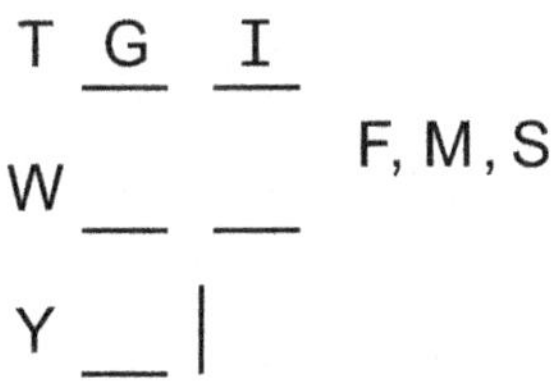

```
T  G  I
            F, M, S
W  __ __

Y  __ |
```

This doesn't work: it violates rule 3. Either the Trents need the stable, or the Yandells need the inn. Here the Trents have the inn.

(The Trents can't take the stable because the Yandells need one building, and the Williamses need two. There are only three buildings remaining.)

So the Williamses need to take the granary and the inn. Note that the Williamses now can't have the forge (rule 2):

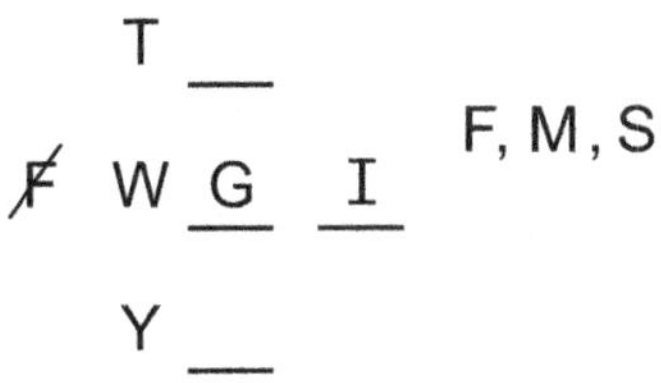

```
     T  __
               F, M, S
not-F  W  G  I

     Y  __
```

Next, apply the remaining rules. The Yandells don't have the inn, so the Trents need the stable (rule 3):

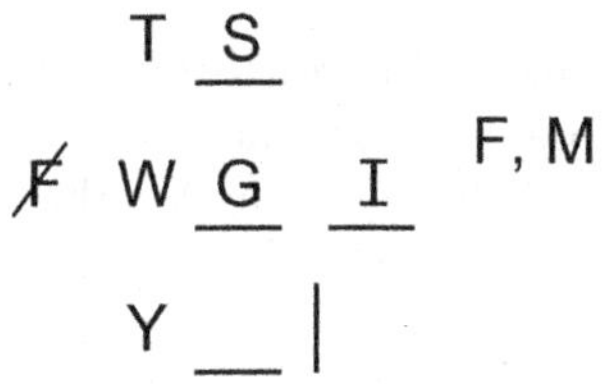

```
     T  S
               F, M
not-F  W  G  I

     Y  __ |
```

The forge and the mill are left. The Yandells take one, and the other building can go with either the Trents or the Williamses. As long as you don't place the forge with the Williamses (rule 2).

You can use the diagram above to eliminate answers. It disproves **A, C, D** and **E.**

B is **CORRECT.**

Question 18

This question says the Trents owned exactly one building. We also know from the setup that the Yandells own one building. So this question has this distribution:

T __ |

W __ __ __ |

Y __ |

The question is asking what buildings the Trents can own. Given this, you should consider what rules affect the Trents. Either they need the stables, or the Yandells need the inn. It's pretty probable the Trents can own the stables, so lets see if we can make a working scenario:

T S |

W I M G |

Y F |

(Note: this is not the *only* scenario where the Trents can own the stable. But it doesn't need to be. We're just trying to prove that it's *possible* for the Trents to own the stables)

Since it's possible for the Trents to own the stables, we're left with only **C** and **E** as potentially correct answers.

C doesn't work. If the Trents have the inn, then rule 3 is broken. The Trents don't have the stables, and the Yandells don't have the inn.

E is CORRECT. There's no need to prove that the Trents could have the forge and the mill, since we know for sure all the other answers are wrong. But for completeness, here are two scenarios that prove **E:**

T F |

W M G S |

Y I |

T M |

W S F G |

Y I |

Game 4 – Floral bouquets
Questions 19–23

Setup

This is a grouping game, oddly similar to the third game. I drew it vertically, like the first question:

1 ___

2 ___

3 ___

I drew a unique diagram to add the rules to this diagram. When a game presents something you've never seen before, you need to innovate. The goal is to make a diagram that's clear and reminds you of the rule. It doesn't need to be "correct" (there is no one correct diagram); your innovated diagram just needs to be *useful*. Here's what I drew:

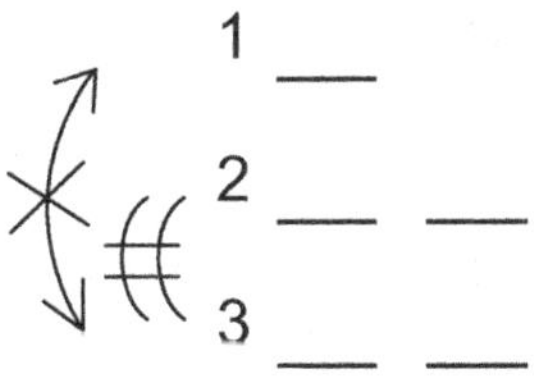

1 ___

2 ___ ___

3 ___ ___

This represents the idea that bouquets 2 and 3 need exactly two flowers in common, and bouquets 1 and 3 cannot have any bouquets in common.

In practice, I memorized these two rules. The lines are just a memory aid. If you go into a game like this *without* memorizing the rules, you're at a severe disadvantage.

Note: I drew these lines on my main diagram, but I did *not* draw them on the diagrams I drew beside each question. In these explanations, I've kept the lines to the left on most diagrams for clarity. But generally your new diagrams should be simpler than the main diagram.

I'm going to draw rules 4 and 5 before rule 3:

Rule 4:

L → R and ~~S~~

S or ~~R~~ → ~~L~~

Rule 5:

T → P

~~P~~ → ~~T~~

I've drawn the contrapositives. On my own game sheet, I did not do this. When you get to an advanced level, you'll be able to see contrapositives in your head. But until that point, you should draw contrapositives.

Finally, rule three says that bouquet 3 has snapdragons. If we combine this with rule 4, we can say that bouquet 3 cannot have lilies:

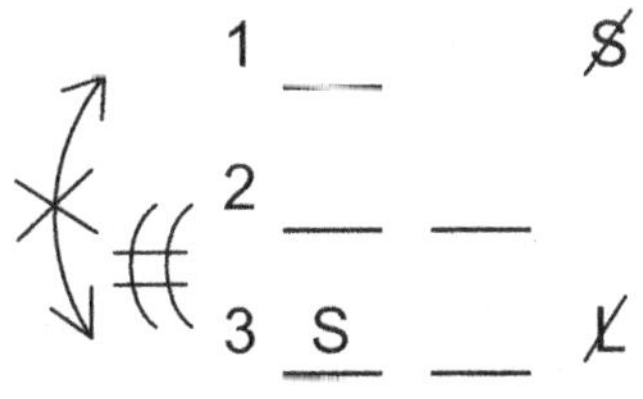

1 ___ ~~S~~

2 ___ ___

3 S ___ ~~L~~

I've also drawn that bouquet 1 cannot have snapdragons. That's due to rule 1: bouquets 1 and 3 cannot have any flowers in common.

Those are all the deductions. As with most modern games, the key to success is simply knowing the rules well and applying them when the questions give you new rules.

Main Diagram

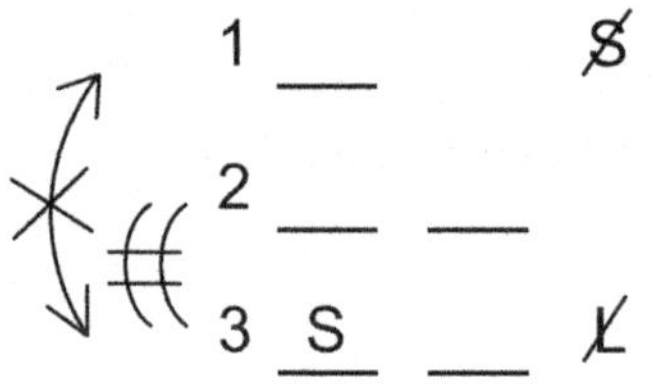

1 ___ S̸
2 ___ ___
3 S ___ L̸

(1) L → R and S̸

S or R̸ → L̸

(2) T → P

P̸ → T̸

Question 19

For acceptable order questions, go through the rules and use them to eliminate answers one by one.

Rule 1 eliminates **B.** Bouquets 1 and 3 cannot have any flowers in common.

Unusually, rule 2 eliminates no answers.

Rule 3 eliminates **E.** Bouquet 3 must have snapdragons.

Rule 4 eliminates **D.** A bouquet can't have lilies and snapdragons.

Rule 5 eliminates **C.** If a bouquet has tulips, then it needs peonies too.

A is **CORRECT.** It violates no rules.

Question 20

This question places lilies in bouquet 1. Whenever a question gives you a new rule, your first task is to think about how this affects the other rules.

Rule 4 says that if there are lilies, then there are roses:

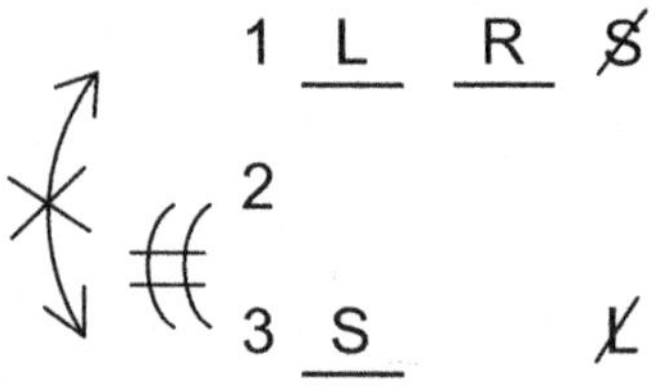

1 L R S̸
2
3 S L̸

Rule 1 says that bouquets 1 and 3 can't share flowers. So bouquet 3 can't have roses:

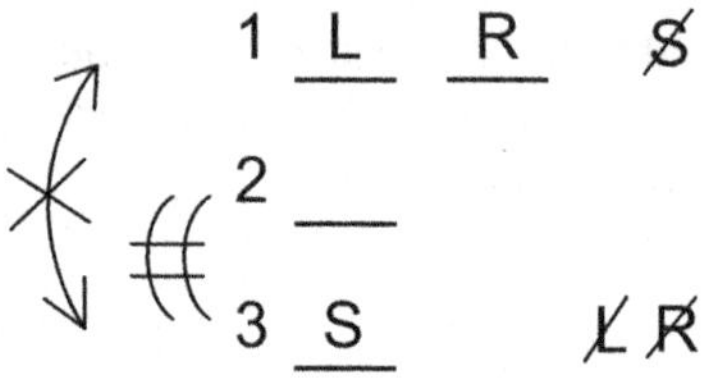

1 L R S̸
2 ___
3 S L̸ R̸

The next deduction is tricky. Bouquets 2 and 3 must share two flowers. So bouquet 3 needs at least one more flower. Who else can go in bouquet 3? T and P are left. We can either place:

- P, or
- T and P (rule 5: if there's T, there's P).

So either way, bouquet 3 has P. **B** is **CORRECT.**

Question 21

This question places tulips in bouquet one. You should ask what other rules that affects. Rule 5 says that if a bouquet has tulips, it needs peonies:

1 T P ~~S~~
2 __
3 S ~~L~~

(Note: I've left off some "not" rules for simplicity. But you should be aware that, due to rule 1, bouquet three can't have T or P, and bouquet 1 can't have S. That's what the double arrow with the X represents)

Rule 1 says that bouquets 1 and 3 don't share flowers. So therefore bouquet 3 can't have tulips or peonies:

1 T P ~~S~~
2 __
3 S ~~T~~ ~~P~~ ~~L~~

Bouquet three now has a lot of restrictions. Whenever that happens, you should ask what variables *can* go in a group. S is already in bouquet 3, and T, P and L can't go there. There are just five flowers, so only roses are left.

Bouquets 2 and 3 must share two flowers each. Bouquet 3's second flower can only be roses, and we must give the same two flowers to bouquet 2:

1 T P ~~S~~
2 S R
3 S R | ~~T~~ ~~P~~ ~~L~~

(The vertical line on group three is just a reminder that that group is full.)

The deduction that bouquets 2 and 3 need S and R answers the question. Only **E** has snapdragons and roses, therefore **E** is **CORRECT.** Just for the sake of completeness, this diagram proves that **E** is possible:

1 T P
2 P R S T
3 S R |

Question 22

When a question mentions a specific group, you should ask what rules apply to that group. This question mentions bouquet 2. From the rules, we know that bouquet 2 needs to share two flowers with bouquet 3.

Therefore, **A** is **CORRECT,** it can't be true.
If bouquet 2 only has lilies and roses, then there aren't two flowers that bouquets 2 and 3 can share. That's because bouquet 3 can't have lilies, because it has snapdragons (rule 4).

Question 23

This was a tricky question. I had to solve it by brute force elimination. We're looking for something that can't be true. So any answer that's possible is wrong. To eliminate an answer, you just need to construct a working scenario that shows it's possible.

I first checked past questions to see if they proved any answers were possible. The correct answer to question 19 proves that **A** is possible.

This diagram from question 21 proves that **B** is possible:

1 T P ~~S~~
2 S R
3 S R | ~~T~~ ~~P~~ ~~L~~

This scenario proves that **D** is possible:

1 L R
2 P R S
3 S P

This scenario proves that **E** is possible:

1 L R
2 P T
3 S P T

Note: Brute force is slower, but it doesn't have to be *slow*. Practice making scenarios quickly. The biggest danger is hesitation. If you know the rules, and draw without hesitating, you can draw a correct scenario in 5-10 seconds.

C is **CORRECT.** Bouquet 2 can't have only L, P and R. This is a little tricky to prove. Let's go step by step. First, place LPR in bouquet 2:

1 __
2 L P R |
~~L~~ 3 S

Next, apply rule 2: bouquets 2 and 3 need two flowers in common. Bouquet 3 can't have lilies, so it must have peonies and roses:

1 __
2 L P R
~~L~~ 3 S P R

Next, apply rule 1: Bouquets 1 and 3 can't share flowers. So bouquet 1 can't have S, P or R:

~~S~~ ~~P~~ ~~R~~ 1 __
2 L P R
~~L~~ 3 S P R

But, bouquet 1 needs at least one flower. And this is why **C** doesn't work. The only flowers left are tulips and lilies. But neither work: tulips require peonies, and lilies require roses.

So **C** is impossible, and therefore **CORRECT.**

Section IV – Logical Reasoning

Question 1

QUESTION TYPE: Weaken

CONCLUSION: Chocolate reduces our ability to taste coffee.

REASONING: 10 people were given coffee. Five of them were given chocolate first. The ones who didn't have chocolate tasted difference in the coffee. The ones who did taste chocolate couldn't taste difference in the coffee.

ANALYSIS: This is a very weak argument. The sample size is very small. Five people is not enough of a sample to draw any conclusion.

The right answer indirectly points this out by using a principle of science: repetition. If a result is valid, we should be able to repeat an experiment and get the same result. In this case, researchers repeated the experiment and got a different result. Likely because the original sample was too small.

A. Random assignment to groups is a *good* thing. This strengthens the argument.
B. If you can repeat an experiment and get the same result, that suggests the result is valid. This strengthens the argument.
C. This is just a random fact about how coffee and chocolate are consumed. This tells us nothing about whether chocolate interferes with our ability to taste chocolate.
D. **CORRECT.** This suggests that the five people who couldn't taste differences simply don't taste differences in coffee under any circumstances. With chocolate, they tasted no difference. Now, without chocolate, they still taste no difference. The likely explanation is that five people is too small a sample size to judge anything.
E. The main point is that the group *did* taste differences. It doesn't really matter how large the difference is. The other group tasted absolutely no difference.

Question 2

QUESTION TYPE: Principle – Strengthen

CONCLUSION: Residents want to stop a landowner from building on a landscape that had been used in a painting by a famous painter.

REASONING: The building would hurt the community's artistic and historic heritage.

ANALYSIS: The family wants to build a house. They have a legal right to do so.

The community has an artistic interest in not having a building built. To support the argument, we need to show that this community interest somehow restricts the family's legal right to built on their property.

A. The passage isn't talking about preserving a historic building! Instead, it's talking about preventing a building from being built.
B. This tells us the community should buy the land. That's no good. We're trying to support the argument that the community has a say in how the land is used even if they don't own it.
C. This principle tells us that the *artist* could ask the landowner not to build a building. But the artist is dead! This is no help.
D. **CORRECT.** In this case, the community does have a historic and artistic interest in not having the new building built. So this answer suggests the family's right to build is constrained.
E. This talks about what the law should say. But the stimulus said there's no law against building a building. So this doesn't help the argument that the landlord still shouldn't build a building.

Question 3

QUESTION TYPE: Flawed Reasoning

CONCLUSION: Sunscreens don't help reduce UV radiation.

REASONING: People who frequently use sunscreen get as much skin cancer as those who don't.

ANALYSIS: This argument sounds persuasive, but it's bad science. To do a proper experiment, you need a control group. You would take 1,000 people, randomly instruct half of them to wear sunscreen, give the other half no instructions, then compare results.

The reason for random assignment is that otherwise there may be relevant differences between those who do and don't wear sunscreen.

For instance, maybe those who spend more time in the sun also use more sunscreen. They get more UV radiation, and are more at risk of skin cancer. If their skin cancer rate isn't higher, then sunscreen is likely reducing UV radiation.

A. The argument wasn't talking about the other effects of sunscreen. This isn't relevant.

B. This is a relevant difference, but we have no reason to expect that the non-sunscreen group had more severe skin cancers.
Absent any other information, we can assume that if two groups have the same number of cancers, then the severity of those cancers is comparable.

C. The stimulus said that all sunscreen is designed to block UV rays. So there are no other sunscreens to consider.

D. It's very possible to challenge the evidence. You'd just have to check the source of the cancer statistics and see if everything checked out. Numbers are either right or wrong: they're easy to challenge.

E. **CORRECT.** This is a relevant difference. If people who use sunscreen spend more time in the sun, they are exposed to more UV radiation. The fact that they don't have more cancer is evidence that sunscreen does block UV rays.

Question 4

QUESTION TYPE: Method of Reasoning

CONCLUSION: It's wrong to say Freudian psychotherapy is effective because of the fact that it's slow and expensive.

REASONING: No one would say a car repair shop is good because it's slow and expensive.

ANALYSIS: This seems like a pretty good argument. It's an argument by analogy. Since most people would accept the conclusion about car repair shops, they'll likely accept the analogous conclusion about Freudian psychotherapy.

There's not much to say about the wrong answers: they didn't happen. Instead of trying to "explain" why they're wrong, I've shown an example of what that method of reasoning would look like if it had happened.

A. The author didn't do this.
Example of method: Some say psychotherapy is effective because it's hard. But anything hard isn't worth doing.

B. The author didn't do this.
Example of method: Some say psychotherapy is effective because it's hard. But actually, psychotherapy isn't hard.

C. **CORRECT.** The conclusion about car repair shops is the analogous statement. Most people would agree with that conclusion. The author hopes we'll think that car repair is comparable to psychotherapy.

D. The author didn't do this.
Example of method: Some say psychotherapy is a good idea because it's hard, and as evidence they say we think learning a language is a good idea because it's hard. But this analogy is wrong: language learning has proven results, whereas psychotherapy has no track record of good results.

E. The author didn't do this.
Example of method: Some say psychotherapy causes increased confidence. But actually, people only go to psychotherapy because they become confident enough to talk about their problems with a stranger.

Question 5

QUESTION TYPE: Identify the Conclusion

CONCLUSION: Biodiversity doesn't require the survival of all current species.

REASONING: Biodiversity requires that all niches be filled, but often a niche can be filled by more than one species.

ANALYSIS: The word "while" is a conclusion indicator. Any statement of opinion, uncertainty or qualification tends to be the conclusion.

Another way of finding the conclusion is asking yourself: why are they telling me this? In this case, the author is trying to convince us that not all species are essential to biodiversity.

A third way to find the conclusion is to ask which statements support other statements, and which are supported. In this case, the second sentence is clearly supporting a claim about biodiversity in general. In particular, the fact that many niches can be filled by multiple species is support for the conclusion that biodiversity does not require that all species survive.

A. CORRECT. See the analysis above.
B. This is context that provides support for the conclusion.
C. This is a qualifying statement used to give context to the conclusion.
D. This is evidence that not all species are necessary.
E. The stimulus didn't mention "the species most indispensable for biodiversity". This can't be the conclusion.

Question 6

QUESTION TYPE: Argument Evaluation

CONCLUSION: Patients taking immune system disorder drugs should take two other drugs:

- Existing drugs that preserve bone mass.
- A new drug that enhances the growth of new bone cells.

REASONING: Drugs that treat immune system disorders also increase the risk of losing bone mass via osteoporosis.

ANALYSIS: Drugs are complicated. They can have unwanted side-effects and dangerous interactions with each other.

To evaluate this argument, we should know about the effects of the new drug and whether it will work with the existing drugs.

A. It doesn't matter how many drugs lead to risk of osteoporosis. We already know that the patients in question have an increased risk from the immune system disorder drugs they're taking.
B. People probably are given the drugs because the drugs are essential for survival. We can assume the patients in question aren't harming themselves for no reason.
C. The conclusion was that patients should take the drugs. So cost is relevant. But this is the wrong question for cost. We care whether the drugs are affordable, not how much they cost relative to another type of drug.
D. This doesn't matter. If the patients are already taking the existing drug, then presumably it's a good idea. It's *mildly* relevant to know how long it's been in use, but this wouldn't be the top question on my mind. We can assume that taking a drug that's part of the standard treatment protocol isn't a crazy, untested action.
(This answer is referring to the existing drug, not the new untested drug.)
E. CORRECT. This is very relevant. If the drug is useless when taken in combination with the other drugs, then there's not much point to taking it.

Question 7

QUESTION TYPE: Principle

CONCLUSION: The concert hall can't fulfill the purpose of a civic building.

REASONING: The concert hall is far from the city center. Therefore it doesn't make the city feel alive or promote social cohesion.

ANALYSIS: The author never tells us what the purpose of a civic building is. Given the example of the art museum, the author seems to be assuming that the purpose of a civic building is encouraging social cohesion. It would be best to state that explicitly – this question could be viewed as a necessary assumption question.

We're looking for the principle on which the author bases their argument. The principle seems to be that the purpose of a civic building is to encourage social cohesion and make the city feel alive.

Several of the wrong answers talk about the wrong thing. The argument is about what makes a good civic building, *if* you build one. The argument is *not* talking about whether we should have civic buildings, what downtown should look like, etc.

A. This contradicts the argument. The author says the concert hall *can't* be a good civic building because it's located on a hill. The author thinks civic buildings should be in dense downtown areas.

B. The author actually didn't say that cities need civic buildings. The argument is about what *makes* a civic building good. That's a different question from whether we need civic buildings.

C. This contradicts the argument. The author says the new concert hall is a bad civic building precisely because it's located on a spectacular hill, rather than in a dense downtown area.

D. The argument is not about designing downtowns. It's about what makes civic buildings good.

E. **CORRECT.** This is consistent with the idea that the concert hall is a bad civic building and the art museum is fulfilling the purpose. We know the concert hall doesn't do these things, and the art museum does.

Question 8

QUESTION TYPE: Most Strongly Supported

FACTS:

1. Fluoride enters groundwater when rain dissolves minerals in the soil that contain fluoride.
2. When all other factors are the same, more fluoride enters groundwater when the soil also has lots of sodium.

ANALYSIS: This stimulus seems complicated, but really there are only two things happening. I simplified the stimulus to two facts.

All we can really conclude is that sodium increases how much fluoride enters the soil during rainfall.

A. This has no support. The first sentence tells us that fluoride-bearing minerals *are* a source of fluoride in groundwater, and the argument doesn't tell us about any other sources.

B. This seems to contradict the first sentence. That sentence says that rainfall causes fluoride to enter groundwater.

C. The stimulus doesn't even mention "sodium-bearing minerals". This answer is trying to confuse you by making up a term that sounds like "fluoride-bearing minerals" in order to make a comparison the stimulus never made.

D. **CORRECT.** This is very well supported. The first sentence says that dissolution is how fluoride enters groundwater. So if more fluoride enters groundwater when sodium is present, then presumably sodium increases fluoride dissolution.

E. Look at the fourth line. Researchers are comparing soils with *the same* concentration of fluoride-bearing minerals. In soils with higher concentrations of sodium, more fluoride enters groundwater, *even though* fluoride concentrations are the same.

Question 9

QUESTION TYPE: Role in Argument

CONCLUSION: It's not likely that Hieronymus Bosch was a member of the Brethren of the Free Spirit.

REASONING: There's no evidence that Bosch was a member, and there's evidence he was a member of a different, mainstream church.

ANALYSIS: This is a strong argument. The author says that there's evidence against Fraenger's argument, and no evidence in favor of Fraenger's argument.

The two statements aren't linked. We don't know why there's evidence Bosch was in a mainstream church. Maybe scholars found church records or letters where Bosch mentions going to church.

The statement that there's no evidence Bosch was a member of the Brotherhood is exactly that: we've found no evidence. It's a negative statement: there is a void of evidence on this point.

The only support for Fraenger's hypothesis is that it would explain Bosch's subject matter. But a hypothesis isn't correct just because it allows a convenient explanation.

A. The author *didn't* say that Fraenger is definitely wrong. They just say Fraenger's conclusion is "unlikely" to be correct.
B. The two claims aren't linked. The fact that there is no evidence Bosch was a member of the brotherhood can't serve as positive evidence Bosch was a member of any other organization. The evidence that Bosch was a member of a church would be something like: church records, letters, tax receipts, etc.
C. The author didn't attack Fraenger personally.
D. **CORRECT.** Fraenger's hypothesis is that Bosch was a member of the Brotherhood. The fact that there's no evidence Bosch was a member demonstrates a serious insufficiency in Fraenger's argument. (Essentially, the author argues that Franeger's evidence is 100% insufficient.)
E. The author didn't say that we can't explain Bosch's work. Fraenger's hypothesis was one explanation, but it's possible that there are other plausible explanations that don't depend on Bosch being a member of the Brotherhood.

Question 10

QUESTION TYPE: Flawed Reasoning

CONCLUSION: This super XL is better than this old vacuum cleaner.

REASONING: The salesman ran both vacuums over the carpet. The super XL went second, and picked up dirt. That was dirt the old vacuum didn't pick up.

ANALYSIS: Door-to-door salesman....does that still exist? Regardless, this is a good trick. The salesman's argument seems convincing.

But normally, when vacuuming, you make multiple passes. You never pick up *all* the dirt. It's possible that if the salesman had run the old vacuum second, it would also have picked up dirt left behind by the Super XL.

For a proper comparison, you need to compare the same thing: The first pass of the old vacuum cleaner on a dirty carpet vs. the first pass of the Super XL on another section of dirty carpet.

A. This sounds good, but you must take it at its weakest. "Dirt remained" could refer to a very, very tiny amount of dirt. No vacuum cleaner ever picks up 100% of dirt.

B. The salesman wasn't saying "this Super XL will be better in five years". He's saying it is better *now*. The future state of the Super XL isn't relevant to a comparison of its present quality.

C. The author didn't say the Super XL is the best. They just said it's better than the old vacuum cleaner.

D. Think about how vacuum cleaners work. On the first pass, they always pick up the most dirt. So a worse vacuum cleaner might pick up more dirt if it went first.
You need to compare apples to apples: First pass to first pass.

E. **CORRECT.** The salesman didn't make a good comparison. The first pass of a vacuum cleaner never picks up all the dirt. The salesman should have compared how much dirt each vacuum cleaner would pick up on the first pass.

Question 11

QUESTION TYPE: Identify the Conclusion

CONCLUSION: It's wrong to say that we shouldn't fix the problem (weaknesses in supply chain) just because the problem will only occur far in the future.

REASONING: It would be wrong for an individual to put off saving for retirement just because the problem (having no money in retirement) is far away.

ANALYSIS: This is an argument by analogy. The author says that it's a mistake to avoid fixing a problem just because the consequences won't appear for a long time. They use the example of retirement to support their conclusion that we should do the same thing in the analogous case of the supply chain.

"But" is a significant word and indicates the author's opinion. The author disagrees with the "some people" who argue we don't need to fix anything yet.

Also note the use of the word "irresponsible". That's a moral judgement. Moral judgements tend to be conclusions.

A. This is the opposing opinion. The author's conclusion is that these people are wrong.

B. **CORRECT.** This is it. See the analysis above.

C. This is the author's evidence. It supports the idea it would be irresponsible not to fix the problem.

D. The author didn't say this. They used an analogy of an individual to prove one specific point: it's irresponsible to avoid fixing a problem just because the consequences won't show up for a while.
But that doesn't mean companies should act like individuals in every respect. Companies don't retire, and they're immortal if well-managed.

E. This is silly. The argument is about what companies should do. Retirement advice was just an analogy.
Also, this advice is nonsense. If you're 60 and haven't saved money, you probably have an *even greater* need to save money.

Question 12

QUESTION TYPE: Most Strongly Supported

FACTS:

1. Worldwide book sales are at their highest level ever.
2. Last year, more cookbooks were sold than before.
3. Most of those cookbooks were meant for non-beginners. This has never happened before.
4. More cookbooks than ever were bought by professional cooks.
5. *Problem-Free Cooking,* a book for beginners, it one of those available on every continent.

ANALYSIS: On the LSAT, some words are more important than others. "Most" is one of those words. This question is testing how well you understand the concept of "more books" and "most of those books".

We know most cookbooks were not meant for first time users, and that this has never happened before. And also, more books were sold than ever.

So we can say that more cookbooks for non-beginners were sold last year than ever before. I'll illustrate with some numbers:

Previous year: 900 books sold, 400 for advanced users. (400/900 is less than most)

Last year: 1,000 books sold, 501 for advanced users. (501/1000 is most)

You could make as many examples as you like, but the advanced users number will always be bigger in the second year, because the number of books sold increased, and so did the portion of books bought by advanced users.

The questions presents a lot of information. It's trying to drown you in details. Focus on key concepts like most, and aim to see what's certain.

A. CORRECT. See the analysis above.

B. This answer wants you to think of *Problem-Free Cooking*. But we don't know if it was best selling. We only know it's available on all continents. A book can be available on all continents without being a best seller.

C. This could be true, but doesn't have to be. Cookbook sales were up last year. So it's possible that more professional *and* more non-professional books were sold, even though a greater percentage of cookbooks were for professionals.

D. We don't know this. We know more cooks bought books. But they might have been a tiny proportional of non-beginner purchasers. Advanced home cooks might be the biggest purchasers of books for non-beginners.

E. We have no idea. A book can be available on all continents without being a best seller.

Question 13

QUESTION TYPE: Necessary Assumption

CONCLUSION: Any methane in Mars' atmosphere must have been released recently.

REASONING: Scientists found methane on Mars in 2003. Methane falls apart when it's hit by UV radiation from the sun.

ANALYSIS: This sounds like a good argument. So before you look at the answers, you should ask "how can this be wrong?".

We know sunlight rapidly destroys methane. So for methane to survive, it must somehow avoid sunlight. The argument is assuming that sunlight reaches all methane and fairly quickly. If that's not true, then some methane might persist in Mars' atmosphere for a long time.

A. It doesn't matter what happened in the past. The argument is talking about whether methane is in the upper atmosphere *now*.

B. CORRECT. If this isn't true, then some methane might still be in the atmosphere.
Negation: Some methane in the upper atmosphere of Mars is never exposed to sunlight.

C. This just mixes together three terms from the argument in an irrelevant way: "methane", "detected", "falls apart". The argument never made any link between detection and falling apart. This is an answer designed to seem plausible only because the terms are familiar.

D. The argument is saying that the methane that was detected *had not yet* been exposed. If it had been exposed to UV radiation, the methane would have fallen apart.
The point of the argument is that the methane that was detected will fall apart, in the future. The author is claiming that methane can exist on Mars, but only for a short time, before it is exposed to UV radiation and dissolves.

E. It doesn't matter what happens on Earth. The argument is about Mars. Maybe Earth's methane is protected from UV radiation by some other factor....but this wouldn't matter even if it were true.

Question 14

QUESTION TYPE: Most Strongly Supported

FACTS:

1. Gasoline exhaust creates environmental problems.
2. Gas prices don't take account of these problems, so these problems don't affect how much people drive.
3. Taxes on gasoline would reflect the environmental cost. People would pollute less.

ANALYSIS: I couldn't prephrase anything from these facts. If you're unable to prephrase a Most Strongly Supported question, you should look over the stimulus a second time to make sure the facts are clear. This clarity will let you go through the answers *much* faster and with fewer errors.

A. I skipped this as soon as I read "should". The stimulus just gave us facts about what is true. Facts can never prove a moral point.

B. It's possible that people will become environmentally aware, but it doesn't have to be true. If gas is expensive, you buy less gas, and pollute less as a result. That will happen even if you don't think about the environment at all.

C. CORRECT. This almost feels like it's repeating the stimulus, but actually it's a combination of facts 2 and 3. Fact three says taxes would lead people to *pollute* less, but it doesn't say why. Fact 2 says higher gas costs cause people to *drive* less. Combining these two ideas leads to this answer choice.

D. This is absurd. You have to take answer choices literally. This answer means that you think of *nothing* but gas costs when you drive. You ignore, for example: do I need to drive anywhere? How much does a car cost? Do I need to do some work, rather than drive around? This answer says the *only* factor in driving is gas cost. Presumably, if gas were free, then you would drive forever, according to this answer.

E. This actually contradicts the stimulus. The stimulus said higher gas taxes will reduce pollution. Probably this happens whether or not consumers think of the environment.

Question 15

QUESTION TYPE: Paradox

PARADOX: Hine's emerald dragonflies are endangered and live in wetlands. The larvae can survive only in water.

Red devil crayfish eat the dragonfly larvae, yet the dragonflies are more likely to have healthy populations in areas with red devil crayfish.

ANALYSIS: On paradox questions, you must first of all think about why the situation is confusing. This one can be summed up as: "crayfish eat dragonflies, yet dragonflies seem to benefit from the presence of crayfish."

You need to find an answer that shows one of two things:

1. How crayfish can help dragonflies, OR
2. How environments that help crayfish also help dragonflies.

A. CORRECT. Emerald dragonfly larvae need water to survive. This shows that crayfish can help dragonfly populations to withstand drought.

B. This doesn't show that crayfish *help* the dragonflies. It just shows that the crayfish hurt the dragonflies less than they possibly could.

C. This makes the situation more confusing. It removes a way that crayfish could have helped dragonflies.

D. This doesn't explain anything. It's just an irrelevant fact about the crayfish. Besides, we would expect crayfish to be more widespread, since the dragonflies are endangered.

E. This is just a random fact about crayfish. It doesn't help explain how crayfish help dragonflies.

Question 16

QUESTION TYPE: Most Strongly Supported

FACTS:

1. Stress often causes high blood pressure.
2. Some people can lower their blood pressure by calming their minds and reducing stress.
3. Most people can calm their minds by exercising.

ANALYSIS: On most strongly supported questions, you must combine facts. The combination doesn't *have* to be true, like a "must be true" question. It just has to "make sense". Here, we see this linkage:

Exercise → calm mind → reduce stress → lower blood pressure

These are *not* conditional statements. The arrows just represent which way the ideas flow. It sounds like it's possible that exercise can lower stress and blood pressure. "Most Strongly Supported" questions can have fuzzy deductions. Forgot the strict logic you may use on more formal question types. (Normally, you can't combine a "most" and a "some" statement like this question does.)

A. This gets things backwards. We know lower stress can lead to lower blood pressure, but the reverse might not be true.

B. We don't know this. The second sentence only said "some" people can do this. It might not be true for "most" people.
The fact that "most" people can calm their mind by exercise can't increase the percentage of people who can lower blood pressure by calming their mind. Those are two different groups.

C. This is too strong. The second sentence only says "some" people can lower their blood pressure by calming their mind. That could be as low as 1%. Maybe lack of exercise only increases blood pressure for those people.

D. This is too....direct. We can say that exercise may lower blood pressure, but it's not a direct effect. There are several steps involved.
If something *directly* affects another thing then there are no intermediate steps.

E. CORRECT. This is fairly well supported. "Some" could be as low as one person, and that seems likely based on the stimulus.

Question 17

QUESTION TYPE: Weaken

CONCLUSION: Soot probably doesn't cause the ailment.

REASONING: In cities with lots of soot, there are usually lots of other pollutants.

ANALYSIS: The argument said there's merely a correlation between the ailment and the soot, and other pollutants are the cause. You're supposed to weaken the argument by showing this correlation is actually significant. There are at least two weak points to the argument:

- The author only showed it's *possible* the other pollutants are the cause. You can weaken the argument by showing they in fact aren't the cause.
- The author only said that soot is *usually* accompanied by other pollutants. There may be cities with soot, but without other pollutants. What happens in those cites?

A. This strengthens the argument. The author wanted to show the other pollutants were the cause. This answer suggests they are, because the ailment occurs even where soot is absent but the other pollutants are present.

B. This would help, *if* we knew that the ailment only occurs where soot is present. But the stimulus didn't say that. The ailment is correlated with soot, but it's possible it exists even without soot.

C. **CORRECT.** This weakens the argument by showing that the ailment exists even when other pollutants aren't there. So perhaps soot is the cause.

D. This is complex, but it doesn't mean anything relevant. I'll explain its meaning with an example.
Example of situation: The pollutants smoog, snarf and blug are all correlated with a certain ailment. Therefore it's possible that both snarf and blug each can cause the ailment.

E. This strengthens the argument. The author is trying to show that soot is *not* the cause. This supports that idea by showing that other pollutants may be the cause.

Question 18

QUESTION TYPE: Flawed Parallel Reasoning

CONCLUSION: It will probably rain before the end of summer.

REASONING: It usually rains a few inches in the valley each summer. This summer there's been no rain, and there's only one week of summer left.

ANALYSIS: This is a bad argument. The author ignores the possibility that this summer is unusual and there's a drought.

Abstractly, the error is: assuming that something will happen just because it hasn't happened yet.

Statistics don't work like that. You aren't "due" to have rain, success, failure, etc. The fact that something hasn't happened in a while *decreases* the odds that it will happen, unless you know it must happen for certain.

A. This is a good argument. It just says there "may" be errors. It's certainly possible errors exist.
To be right, this answer should have said there "probably" will be errors.

B. This is a good argument. Errors are unlikely even in a whole issue. So errors are even less likely in a few pages of an issue.

C. **CORRECT.** This takes evidence from what's true on average and assumes it must always happen. But the lack of errors so far makes it *less* likely there are errors in the final pages.
"A few errors on average" could mean that many issues have no errors, and some issues have many errors. Averages aren't evenly distributed.

D. This is a good argument. If there are rarely errors in an entire issue, then it's even less likely there will be errors in a few pages of an issue.

E. It's hard to say if this argument is good or bad. We'd need to know more about Aisha's proofreading skills to be sure. Either way, this argument isn't obviously bad like the stimulus. If there are usually errors, then it is odd that Aisha found none in the entire issue.
The correct answer is different in that it talks about finding errors in a few pages. That's far less likely.

Question 19

QUESTION TYPE: Necessary Assumption

CONCLUSION: We should try to keep children motivated by helping them believe better futures are possible.

REASONING: Young people believe it's impossible to reduce pollution, poverty and war. People lose motivation to work on things they think are impossible.

ANALYSIS: This is a necessary assumption question. I found this one difficult to prephrase. If you don't know what the answer is going to be, you should do three things:

1. Look carefully at the conclusion and reasoning so that you know how they fit together. This lets you spot weak points.
2. See which answers mention a couple of terms from the argument.
3. Negate those answers to see if they lead to the conclusion.

Now that I've reviewed the question, I realized that the author never said that belief in a better future will lead to motivation. They just assumed it would, which is why B is the answer. But in timed conditions, the negation test let me figure that out even when I couldn't predict the answer.

A. This gets things backwards. The author said we should make people believe in a better future in order to motivate them. The reverse assumption isn't necessary.
B. CORRECT. The negation wrecks the argument. **Negation:** Letting people believe in a better future will not improve their motivation.
C. This is a value judgment. The stimulus was about facts: will young people lose motivation, or will they not lose motivation?
D. This isn't necessary. The author only wants young people to *try*. It would be nice if they succeed in ending problems, but the main thing is to make an effort.
E. It doesn't matter why current problems exist. The stimulus is only about whether we can motivate youth *now*.

Question 20

QUESTION TYPE: Strengthen

CONCLUSION: The leakage of glutamate from nerve cells is a cause of long term brain damage from strokes.

REASONING: Glutamate can harm nerve cells if it leaks.

ANALYSIS: This is a complicated question. There are at least two gaps in the argument.

1. The author hasn't shown that elevated glutamate after a stroke comes from leakages in the brain. The author only said glutamate damages nerve cells when it leaks. If glutamate is elevated for other reasons (e.g. diet) it might be harmless.
2. The author hasn't shown that strokes lead to glutamate leakage. It's possible a third factor causes both glutamate leakage and strokes.

The right answer patched over the first weakness: it shows that elevated glutamate comes from leakages.

A. It doesn't matter what other neurotransmitters do. The argument is only talking about glutamate, and we already know that glutamate can damage nerve cells.
B. It doesn't matter if other chemical levels are unusual after a stroke. The argument could work even if glutamate is the only unusual chemical.
C. It doesn't matter what other neurotransmitters do. So this answer adds nothing as we already knew glutamate can leak.
D. CORRECT. This doesn't prove the argument correct, but it strengthens it. It eliminates the possibility that glutamate is elevated due to a different reason, such as a dietary excess of glutamate. This therefore shows that excess glutamate can cause damage in the brain because it's leaking from cells in the brain.
E. This doesn't matter. Not *all* nerve cells are going to leak glutamate at once. So glutamate could leak from cells that die, and then that glutamate could harm other living cells.

Question 21

QUESTION TYPE: Parallel Reasoning

CONCLUSION: Amanda's next song probably won't have more than three chords if it's not a blues song.

REASONING: Amanda has only written punk rock and blues songs. Most punk songs don't have more than three chords.

ANALYSIS: This isn't a rock solid argument, but it's fairly well supported. The author ignores a third possibility: Amanda might write a song that isn't punk or blues. But since Amanda has never done that, it's unlikely.

To parallel this argument, you need to match the structure. A formal diagram isn't useful, but you should be clear on the elements.

1. All have been either A or B
2. B is usually not Y
3. If next one is not A, then probably not Y.

In practice, I skimmed the answers and eliminated those that obviously differed from the structure above. Then I focussed more closely on the two that seemed to match (C and E).

All of the answers use the same terms. They refer to a family named the Guptas, who own pets: parrots and fish. The parrots are noisy.

Despite the similar subject matter, all of the answers are different. Questions like this reward you for focussing on structural factors.

Note that there are many ways of phrasing the idea that all pets owned by the Guptas were fish or parrots. The answers all phrase this idea in different ways, but the statements are logically equivalent.

A. This has the wrong structure. It should have said "If the next is *not A*".
  1. All have been either A or B
  2. B is usually Y.
  3. If the next is B, it will probably be Y.

B. This has the wrong structure. It should have said "if not A, probably Y".
  1. All have been either A or B
  2. B is usually Y.
  3. If Y, probably B.

C. This is close, but it's not quite the same. E is better. This doesn't say "the next". Instead, it's talking about all pets.
  1. All have been either A or B
  2. B is usually Y.
  3. Any that is not A will probably Y.

D. This has the wrong structure.
  1. All have been either A or B
  2. B is usually Y.
  3. If next is not B, probably not Y.

E. **CORRECT.** This matches exactly.
  1. Either A or B.
  2. B is usually Y.
  3. If next one is not A, it will probably be Y.

Note: The fact that the stimulus said "not involve" and this said "will be noisy" is not significant. Putting things in terms of "not" isn't a structural issue, since you can put any "not" statement in a positive form. For example, you could say "noisy" = "not quiet."

Don't focus on words like "not". Focus instead on whether a key term was or was not negated. In this argument, Y wasn't negated in the stimulus or in the correct answer.

Question 22

QUESTION TYPE: Paradox

PARADOX: Advertising affects yogurt preferences more than it affects milk preferences.

Yet when LargeCo advertised its store-brands, sales of store-brand milk increased faster than store-brand yogurt.

ANALYSIS: We would ordinarily expect an ad campaign to increase yogurt sales more than it increases milk sales. But after this ad campaign, milk sales increased more. There are at least two ways to explain this:

1. Some unique factor in the ad campaign made it relatively more effective for milk.
2. Some outside factor increased milk sales or decreased yogurt sales. (Ads are not the only reason products sell)

To properly explain the paradox, you need an answer that shows a *difference* between milk and yogurt. Only D and E do this. On paradox questions, most answers can be eliminated for similar reasons.

A. This doesn't help, because it doesn't tell us anything about milk. We need an answer that explains a *difference* between milk and yogurt.
B. Who cares? The question is asking about the changes in yogurt and milk sales. We only care about why people buy each product. It doesn't matter if people buy yogurt and milk together or separately.
C. This doesn't let us distinguish between milk and yogurt. Both are dairy products.
D. CORRECT. This is a good explanation. It shows that the ad campaign wasn't the only factor in yogurt sales. So it's possible that the ad campaign helped yogurt more than it helped milk, but the nationwide drop in yogurt sales wiped out much of the benefits of the ad campaign.
E. This makes the situation more confusing. The ad campaign shouldn't have affected milk sales if people mainly buy milk based on price. We're not told that milk prices changed.

Question 23

QUESTION TYPE: Principle

PROBLEM: Congratulate → misrepresent
~~Congratulate~~ → hurt feelings

PRINCIPLE:

Insincere → Know they prefer kindness to honesty
~~Know they prefer kindness to honesty~~ → ~~Insincere~~

ANALYSIS: On principle/problem questions, you need to be a robot. You need to look at *exactly* what a rule says and then obey it.

We have just *one* situation where insincerity is allowed. If you *know* that someone prefers kindness to honesty, then you might be allowed to lie to them.

If you *don't* know that (or if you're unsure), then you must be honest.

Shayna doesn't know whether Daniel prefers kindness to honesty. So she must be sincere. She can't congratulate Daniel, even though not congratulating him will hurt his feelings.

A. This doesn't work. If Shayna congratulates Daniel, she will misrepresent her feelings. That's only allowed if she knows for a fact that Daniel prefers kindness to honesty.
B. The fact that Daniel *might* prefer kindness to honesty isn't enough. Shayna would need to know for sure that Daniel feels that way before she misrepresents herself.
C. This is close, but Shayna's beliefs about kindness vs. honesty aren't the issue. What's relevant is what Shayna thinks *Daniel* believes.
D. This doesn't match the principle. Hurt feelings aren't relevant. The *only* reason to lie is if you think the other person would prefer kindness to honesty.
In this case, Daniel might prefer the harsh truth to a gentle lie.
E. CORRECT. If Shayna doesn't know what Daniel wants, the principle says she should be honest.

Question 24

QUESTION TYPE: Sufficient Assumption

CONCLUSION: Democracies need good news media.

Democracy → Media

REASONING: Democracies need a knowledgeable electorate. Electorates can't be knowledgeable without unbiased information about the government.

Democracy → knowledgeable electorate → unbiased information

ANALYSIS: Sufficient assumption questions are very formulaic. You can follow a three step process.

1. Identify the conclusion and split it apart.
2. Attach the evidence onto the parts of the conclusion.
3. Spot the gap. This will be the answer.

Democracy   Media

Democracy → knowledgeable electorate → unbiased information   Media

The gap is between unbiased information and the media.

A. This gets things backwards. The argument said democracies require media, but that doesn't mean that media always lead to democracy.
B. This just reverses one of the statements from the argument. It doesn't help show that unbiased information requires the media.
C. This just reverses the evidence we already have. It doesn't help us prove anything about media.
Knowledgeable electorate → democracy
D. This is just a weird statement. It says that democracy will fail if people encounter any biased information. That's crazy! Virtually all democracies would fail if that's true.
More to the point, this doesn't let us connect the reasoning to the need for media.
E. **CORRECT.** This fills the gap.
Unbiased information → media.

Question 25

QUESTION TYPE: Flawed Reasoning

CONCLUSION: Roberta is probably irritable.

REASONING: Irritable → Tired
Lose things → Tired

Roberta lost her keys.

ANALYSIS: The argument has correctly shown that Roberta is tired. She lost her keys, so we definitely know she's tired.

Being tired is a *necessary* condition for being irritable. But it's not a sufficient condition. Roberta might not be irritable, even though she's tired.

The fact about yawning is irrelevant to Roberta being tired. Knowing that Roberta lost her keys is enough on it's own.

A. The argument never said that yawning is correlated to tiredness. This is a nonsense answer.
B. This refers to circular reasoning. That didn't happen.
Example of flaw: Roberta must be tired, because she must be tired.
C. This is a different flaw.
Example of flaw: Roberta only loses her keys when tired. So all people must lose their keys only when tired.
D. This is almost right. The argument did take a necessary condition for a sufficient condition. But it was a necessary condition for irritability, not for losing keys. This answer refers to the wrong term.
This answer was designed to trap you if you were rushing and just looking for necessary/sufficient.
E. **CORRECT.** See the analysis above.

Question 26

QUESTION TYPE: Necessary Assumption

CONCLUSION: Using genetically modified (GMO) crops will help wildlife.

REASONING: GMO crops don't need pesticides, and pesticides sprayed on crops hurt wildlife.

ANALYSIS: The author is assuming that the GMO crops won't harm wildlife, or will harm them less than pesticides do.

A. **CORRECT.** If this isn't true, then GMO crops will not be better than pesticides.
Negation: GMO crops will cause at least as much harm as pesticides.

B. This is a silly statement. "Even slightly" could mean one micro-gram less pesticides. This sort of answer could never impact anything.

C. It doesn't matter if GMO crops are never sprayed with pesticides. It only matters whether they are sprayed less often.
Negation: GMO crops are sprayed with pesticides, but only 0.000000001% as much as regular crops.

D. It doesn't matter how much crops cost. Cost would affect whether GMO crops are used, but the stimulus is only about what happens *if* they are used. That's a different question.

E. Ugh, what a complex answer.
We're trying to prove that GMO crops will help. This answer adds a necessary condition for GMO crops helping. That's no good. Adding an extra necessary condition makes it *harder* to do something.

Appendix: LR Questions By Type

Strengthen

Section II, #22
Section IV, #20

Weaken

Section II, #9
Section II, #19
Section IV, #1
Section IV, #17

Sufficient Assumption

Section II, #10
Section II, #12
Section IV, #24

Parallel Reasoning

Section II, #17
Section IV, #21

Flawed Parallel Reasoning

Section II, #7
Section IV, #18

Necessary Assumption

Section II, #1
Section II, #8
Section II, #20
Section IV, #13
Section IV, #19
Section IV, #26

Method of Reasoning

Section II, #14
Section II, #16
Section IV, #4

Must Be True

Section II, #21

Most Strongly Supported

Section II, #23
Section IV, #8
Section IV, #12
Section IV, #14
Section IV, #16

Paradox

Section II, #2
Section II, #24
Section IV, #15
Section IV, #22

Principle

Section II, #4
Section II, #6
Section IV, #2
Section IV, #7
Section IV, #23

Identify The Conclusion

Section II, #11
Section IV, #5
Section IV, #11

Argument Evaluation

Section IV, #6

Complete the Argument

Section II, #25

Role in Argument

Section IV, #9

Flawed Reasoning

Section II, #3
Section II, #5
Section II, #13
Section II, #15
Section II, #18
Section IV, #3
Section IV, #10
Section IV, #25

Thank You

First of all, thank you for buying this book. Writing these explanations has been the most satisfying work I have ever done. I sincerely hope they have been helpful to you, and I wish you success on the LSAT and as a lawyer.

If you left an Amazon review, you get an extra special thank you! I truly appreciate it. You're helping others discover LSAT Hacks.

Thanks also to Anu Panil, who drew the diagrams for the logic games. Anu, thank you for making sense of the scribbles and scans I sent you. You are surely ready to master logic games after all the work you did.

Thanks to Alison Rayner, who helped me with the layout and designed the cover. If this book looks nice, she deserves credit. Alison caught many mistakes I would never have found by myself (any that remain are my own, of course).

Thanks to Ludovic Glorieux, who put up with me constantly asking him if a design change looked good or bad.

Finally, thanks to my parents, who remained broadly supportive despite me being crazy enough to leave law school to teach the LSAT. I love you guys.

About The Author

Graeme Blake lives in Montreal Canada. He first took the LSAT in June 2007, and scored a 177. It was love at first sight. He taught the LSAT for Testmasters for a couple of years before going to the University of Toronto for law school.

Upon discovering that law was not for him, Graeme began working as an independent LSAT tutor. He teaches LSAT courses in Montreal for Ivy Global and tutors students from all around the world using Skype.

He publishes a series of LSAT guides and explanations under the title LSAT Hacks. Versions of these explanations can be found at LSAT Blog, Cambridge LSAT and LSAT Hacks, as well as amazon.com.

Graeme is also the moderator of www.reddit.com/r/LSAT, Reddit's LSAT forum. He worked for a time with 7Sage LSAT.

Graeme finds it unusual to write in the third person to describe himself, but he recognizes the importance of upholding publishing traditions. He wonders if many people read about the author pages.

You can find him at www.lsathacks.com and www.reddit.com/r/LSAT.

Graeme encourages you to get in touch by email, his address is graeme@lsathacks.com. Or you can call 514-612-1526. He's happy to hear feedback or give advice.

Further Reading

I hope you liked this book. If you did, I'd be very grateful if you took two minutes to review it on amazon. People judge a book by its reviews, and if you review this book you'll help other LSAT students discover it.

Ok, so you've written a review and want to know what to do next.

The most important LSAT books are the preptests themselves. Many students think they have to read every strategy guide under the sun, but you'll learn the most simply from doing real LSAT questions and analyzing your mistakes.

At the time of writing, there are 73 official LSATs. The most recent ones are best, but if you've got a while to study I recommend doing every test from 19 or from 29 onwards.

This series (LSAT Hacks) is a bit different from other LSAT prep books. This book is not a strategy guide.

Instead, my goal is to let you do what my own students get to do when they take lessons with me: review their work with the help of an expert.

These explanations show you a better way to approach questions, and exactly why answers are right or wrong.

If you found this book useful, here's the list of other books in the series:

(Note – the series was formerly titled "Hacking the LSAT" so the older books still have that title until I update them)

- Hacking The LSAT: Full Explanations For LSATs 29-38, Volume I
- Hacking The LSAT: Full Explanations For LSATs 29-38, Volume II
- Explanations for '10 Actual Official LSATs Volume V' – Volume I, LSATs 62-66
- Explanations for '10 Actual Official LSATs Volume V' – Volume I, LSATs 67-71
- LSAT 72 Explanations (LSAT Hacks Series)

Keep an eye out, as I'll be steadily publishing explanations for other LSATs.

If you *are* looking for strategy guides, try Manhattan LSAT or Powerscore. Unlike other companies, they use real LSAT questions in their books.

I've written a longer piece on LSAT books on Reddit. It includes links to the best LSAT books and preptests. If you're serious about the LSAT and want the best materials, I strongly recommend you read it:

http://redd.it/uf4uh

(this is a shortlink that takes you to the correct page)

Free LSAT Email Course

This book is just the beginning. It teaches you how to solve individual questions, but it's not designed to give you overall strategies for each section.

There's so much to learn about the LSAT. As a start, I've made a free, five day email course. Each day I'll send you an email teaching you what I know about a subject.

LSAT Email Course Overview

- Intro to the LSAT
- Logical Reasoning
- Logic Games
- Reading Comprehension
- How to study

What people say about the free LSAT course

These have been awesome. More please!!! - **Cailie**

Your emails are tremendously helpful. - **Matt**

Thanks for the tips! They were very helpful, and even make you feel like you studied a bit. Great insight and would love more! - **Haj**

Sign up for the free LSAT email course here

http://lsathacks.com/email-course/

p.s. I've had people say this free email course is more useful than an entire Kaplan course they took. It's 100% free. Good luck - Graeme

Made in the USA
Monee, IL
07 July 2026